Business Models for the Circular Economy

OPPORTUNITIES AND CHALLENGES FOR POLICY

Please cite this publication as:
OECD (2019), *Business Models for the Circular Economy: Opportunities and Challenges for Policy*, OECD Publishing, Paris.
https://doi.org/10.1787/g2g9dd62-en

ISBN 978-92-64-31141-1 (print)
ISBN 978-92-64-31142-8 (pdf)

Photo credits: Cover © Billion Photos/Shutterstock.com.

Corrigenda to OECD publications may be found on line at: *www.oecd.org/about/publishing/corrigenda.htm*.

Foreword

Recent decades have seen an unprecedented growth in demand for natural resources and the materials derived from them. Around 80 billion tonnes of minerals, fossil fuels, and biomass were fed into the global economy in 2011, and this is only likely to increase with population growth and improved standards of living. OECD modelling indicates that resource use may more than double by 2060 under business as usual.

Continued depletion of the planet's natural resource stock will have a number of economic and environmental consequences. First, ongoing harvesting of mineral ores, fossil fuel reserves, and agricultural land will tend to place upwards pressure on resource prices, affecting resource access and economic development. Second, resource depletion in some countries, and the resulting concentration of supply in others, will tend to increase the likelihood of geo-politically related supply shocks. Third, the environmental pressures associated with the extraction, use, and disposal of natural resources will probably grow, with adverse impacts on quality of life as well as future economic growth.

These issues have sparked recent interest in how to decouple economic activity from natural resource use and their environmental impacts. Improved resource efficiency and a transition to a more circular economy are seen as key ways forward. Many countries have launched national circular economy, resource efficiency, or sustainable materials management roadmaps. Resource efficiency has also been included in the G7 and G20 agendas, as well as being central to the 2030 Agenda for Sustainable Development.

In practice, decoupling can be pursued along several pathways, including improved productivity at the firm level and a shift towards services. However, achieving real progress will also require that greener modes of production and consumption – circular business models as they are called in this report – gain a greater foothold in our economies. The traditional linear model of resource extraction, product ownership, and eventual disposal is unlikely to deliver the sustainable future that we want.

Business Models for a Circular Economy: Opportunities and Challenges from a Policy Perspective has been developed by the Environmental Policy Committee's Working Party on Resource Productivity and Waste. The report addresses the key characteristics, potential scalability, and likely environmental impacts of five headline circular business models. The use of renewable materials in manufacturing, the recycling and remanufacturing of end of life products, and the sharing and leasing of already existing assets are all considered. By identifying the factors that are currently hindering the broader adoption of circular business models, this report can help to support policy efforts to transition to a more resource efficient and circular economy.

Rodolfo Lacy, Director, Environment, OECD

Acknowledgements

This report has been authored by Andrew McCarthy, Matthias Helf, and Peter Börkey of the OECD Environment Directorate. The authors are grateful to delegates of the Working Party on Resource Productivity and Waste for helpful comments on earlier drafts of this paper. They would also like to thank Frithjof Laubinger for his substantive inputs and the editing of the publication and Ruben Bibas for his advice and feedback. Laura Dockings and Soojin Jeong provided editorial assistance. The authors are responsible for any remaining omissions or errors.

Work on this report was conducted under the overall supervision of Shardul Agrawala, Head of the Environment and Economy Integration Division of the OECD's Environment Directorate.

Finally, this work would not have been possible without the generous financial support of Japan, Germany, Korea, The Netherlands and Switzerland.

Table of contents

Tables

Figures

Boxes

Abbreviations and acronyms

B2B	Business to Business
B2C	Business to Consumer
C2C	Consumer to Consumer
C2B	Consumer to Business
CMS	Chemical Management Services
ESCO	Energy Service Company
GHG	Greenhouse Gases
GWP	Global Warming Potential
IPM	Integrated Pest Management
LCA	Lifecycle Assessment
MRF	Material Recovery Facility
OEM	Original Equipment Manufacturer
PSS	Product Service Systems
TEU	Total Energy Use
VKT	Vehicle Kilometres Travelled

Executive Summary

Natural resources, and the materials derived from them, represent the physical basis for the economic system. Recent decades have witnessed an unprecedented growth in demand for these resources. This has triggered interest from policymakers in transitioning to a more resource efficient and circular economy.

The present report focusses on the current scale and possible environmental impacts of five business models that could support the transition to a more resource efficient and circular economy. Each business model modifies the pattern of product and material flows through the economy. By doing so, they have the potential to reduce the environmental pressures that result from current systems of production and consumption. The exact mechanisms vary:

- Circular supply models replace traditional material inputs derived from virgin resources with bio-based, renewable, or recovered materials, which reduces demand for virgin resource extraction in the long run
- Resource recovery models recycle waste into secondary raw materials, thereby diverting waste from final disposal while also displacing the extraction and processing of virgin natural resources
- Product life extension models extend the use period of existing products, slow the flow of constituent materials through the economy, and reduce the rate of resource extraction and waste generation
- Sharing models facilitate the sharing of under-utilised products, and can therefore reduce demand for new products and their embedded raw materials
- Product service system models, where services rather than products are marketed, improve incentives for green product design and more efficient product use, thereby promoting a more sparing use of natural resources

Not all of these business models are necessarily new. Recycling, reuse, and repair have existed for millennia. The sharing of under-utilised household possessions also has a long history, and the provision of access to products, rather than ownership of them, is not so different from traditional product leasing. What is new is the growing diversity and sophistication of these business models, as well as the range of sectors they are adopted in.

The market share held by these business models is small but there is considerable room for future scale up. In most sectors, the market penetration of circular business models remains limited and is usually no more than 5 to 10% in economic terms. Although some business models have experienced rapid recent growth, much of this has been from a very low base, and has been confined to a handful of economic niches. Consequently, there remains considerable potential for the scale up of circular economy business models, both within and across sectors.

Some circular business models are more amenable to more widespread adoption than others. Waste recycling and product reuse and repair, for instance, have a long history and are relatively mature. Achieving higher rates of market penetration for these more mature circular business models will require significant changes to existing policy frameworks. In some instances, this is already happening; the recent adoption of a comprehensive strategy on plastics in the European Union is one such example.

There are a number of other business models that have appeared more recently, and are scaling up rapidly. Technological innovations along with an increased consumer willingness to pay for green products seem to have been important drivers. For sharing models, and for certain variants of product service system models, for instance, the emergence of the internet, mobile phone technology, and the development of referral and reputational systems have allowed certain products to be shared more widely than ever before. Airbnb has gone from being a curiosity in the accommodation sector ten years ago to being the largest single supplier of short-term stays today. Similarly, global membership of urban car sharing schemes is growing at an annual rate of up to 65%.

More widespread adoption of circular business models would significantly reduce environmental pressures, although there is uncertainty about possible rebound effects. The information compiled in this report allows three main conclusions to be drawn on the environmental implications of broader circular business model adoption:

- Insights from the lifecycle assessment literature indicate that the environmental footprint of circular products and services are typically significantly smaller than that for traditional products, which could have important first order environmental benefits.
- These first order benefits will not be evenly distributed across the product lifecycle. For example, remanufacturing reduces emissions and environmental pressures upstream associated with resource extraction, whereas sharing and product service system models also reduce pressures associated with the product use-phase.
- The overall environmental impact will also depend on indirect economic spillover and feedback effects. For example, in the context of sharing models, it has been shown that Airbnb rooms are typically 15 – 20% cheaper than equivalent hotel rooms. The consumer savings that this generates may well be allocated to additional consumption, which may partially or fully offset first order environmental gains.

In order to realise the environmental benefits, policy frameworks will need to evolve to create the conditions for wider uptake of circular business models. Ultimately, achieving a genuine transition to a more circular economy will be unlikely if circular business models continue to occupy small economic niches. Policy can play an important role by addressing the market failures, policy misalignments and status quo biases that currently hinder the competitiveness of these business models, including:

- ensuring that the full environmental costs of production and consumption activities are reflected in market prices;
- improving collaboration within and across sectoral value chains, through e.g. fostering industrial symbiosis clusters, promoting online material marketplaces or establishing secondary raw material certification schemes, and, more generally, facilitation of cooperation within;

- ensuring that existing regulatory frameworks are coherent and fit for purpose, and not serving to preserve an existing status quo;
- improving existing educational and information programs to provide individuals with a better understanding of the unintended consequences of their consumption choices (e.g. behavioural insights and nudges);
- promoting the supply of circular products ("supply-push measures") or demand for them ("demand-pull measures"). For the former this includes eco-design standards, strengthened extended producer responsibility (EPR) schemes, and the provision of targeted R&D funding. Examples of the latter include differentiated VAT rates, recycled content mandates, and product labelling standards.

Chapter 1. Introduction

This chapter sets out the motivation for the development of this report. It notes the rapid growth of resource extraction, use and disposal that has taken place in recent years, and the adverse environmental impacts that are occurring as a result. Improved resource efficiency and a transition to a more circular economy are then highlighted as potential solutions to these issues: using natural resources relatively sparingly would allow economic growth to be decoupled from its less desirable environmental side-effects. The chapter concludes by identifying the more widespread adoption of circular business models as a concrete means of achieving decoupling.

Recent decades have witnessed an unprecedented growth in demand for resources. This has been driven by the rapid industrialisation of emerging economies and continued high levels of material consumption in developed countries. As a result, the weight of materials consumed worldwide has more than doubled since 1980, and increased ten-fold since 1900. By 2060, the world population is expected to increase from about 7 billion to about 10 billion (UN, 2017[1]). At the same time, per capita income of the world's population is expected to roughly triple (OECD, 2019[2]). This will substantially increase demand for natural resources, especially if global production and consumption patterns converge with those of OECD countries. OECD modelling indicates that global primary materials use may more than double from 79 Gt in 2011 to 167 Gt in 2060, if existing trends continue (OECD, 2019[2]).

Continued rapid growth in natural resource use will have several economic and environmental consequences. First, ongoing harvesting of the highest quality mineral ores, fossil fuel reserves, and areas of agricultural land will tend to stimulate higher resource prices, with potentially negative consequences for resource access and economic development.[1] Second, resource depletion in some countries, and the resulting concentration of supply in others, will tend to increase the likelihood of geo-politically related supply shocks. This may begin to represent a considerable operational risk for manufacturing firms with relatively one dimensional supply chains. Third, the environmental pressures generated by the extraction, processing, and disposal of natural resources will continue to weigh upon the planet's sink capacity and, in some cases, become a constraint on economic activity. At the firm level, the threat of climate or other environmental regulation will become a significant business risk for resource intensive or polluting firms.

These concerns have led to increased interest in how to decouple economic activity from resource inputs and the generation of polluting by-products (Box 1.1). Promoting improved resource efficiency has become a major focus at the international level, and a succession of multilateral initiatives and frameworks have been introduced. An OECD Council Recommendation issued in 2008 encouraged member countries to "take appropriate actions to improve resource productivity and reduce negative environmental impacts of materials and product use". In the same year, G8 environment ministers signed the Kobe 3R Action Plan, in which countries agreed to prioritise implementation of 3Rs policy in order to improve resource productivity. There have also been several important recent developments. The creation of the G7 Alliance on Resource Efficiency at Schloss Elmau in 2015, and the subsequent adoption of the Toyama Framework on Material Cycles, signalled increasing interest from G7 countries. The inclusion of specific goals related to resource efficiency in the 2030 Agenda for Sustainable Development also represented a major landmark. Finally, the introduction of resource efficiency into the G20 agenda in 2017 was notable, particularly given the presence in that forum of various countries with large resource endowments.

At the national level, transitioning to a more circular economy is also receiving considerable attention. Circular economy roadmaps have been introduced in the People's Republic of China (hereafter China) in 2013, in the European Union in 2015, and in Finland, France, the Netherlands, and Scotland in 2016. Other countries have introduced national level policy frameworks with different names, but with largely similar objectives. Japan's Fundamental Law for Establishing a Sound Material-Cycle Society and the United States' Sustainable Materials Management Program Strategic Plan are two such examples.

Box 1.1. The potential benefits of a transition to a more resource efficient and circular economy

The transition to a more resource efficient and circular economy is not usually considered to be a policy goal in itself. Rather, it is the economic, environmental, and social gains that might accompany such a transition that seem to be of interest for governments. Specific benefits that are often cited include, (i) a reduction in the environmental pressures – greenhouse gas emissions, particulate pollution, toxicity, biodiversity loss etc – arising from current systems of production and consumption, (ii) economic expansion and job creation driven by the emergence of new opportunities in certain sectors, and (iii) reduced risk of raw material supply shocks either in the short term (due to geo-political factors), or in the longer term (due to natural resource depletion).

There is an emerging body of work that uses macroeconomic modelling tools to assess the second issue – that relating to economic growth and employment. The majority of existing modelling assessments find that a policy driven transition to a more resource efficient and circular economy could take place with (potentially significant) positive impacts on economic growth (McCarthy, Dellink and Bibas, 2018[3]). That said, this literature is rather limited in scope, and often includes ad-hoc assumptions that are overly optimistic. Ongoing modelling work at the OECD and elsewhere is beginning to address these issues.

This report addresses the first issue – the reductions in environmental pressure that could result from a circular economy transition. It focusses on the key activities – or business models – that will be required to drive such a transition, and assesses their scalability and environmental footprint relative to traditional (or "linear") equivalents. The firm level approach taken in this report is intended to serve as a complement to the macroeconomic modelling work discussed above.

In practice, there are various channels through which decoupling, improved resource efficiency, or the transition to a more circular economy can be achieved. At the aggregate level, decoupling could result from changes in the structure of the economy; a demand driven increase in the share of services in total output for example. At the level of individual production facilities, decoupling could result from technologically driven improvements in resource productivity; incremental improvements in the proportion of metal recovered from mineral ores for example. A third channel, and the one that represents the main focus of this report, involves "circular modes of production" or, put differently, activities that use virgin non-renewable resources (and the materials derived from them) relatively sparingly.

Box 1.2. Definitions in this report: resource efficiency, the circular economy, and circular business models

Resource efficiency is used by UNEP (2017[4]) to refer to a set of ideas including: (i) the technical efficiency of resource use, (ii) resource productivity, or the extent to which economic value is added to a given quantity of resources, and (iii) the extent to which resource extraction or use has negative impacts on the environment. In concrete terms, resource efficiency, or more precisely resource intensity, can be calculated as the ratio between the value of economic output from a particular sector or economy, and the amount of resources (typically in terms of weight) used to produce it. An improvement in resource efficiency therefore describes a situation where more economic value is being produced with a particular amount of resources (or one where fewer resources are being used).

There is no single accepted definition of the circular economy, although a comparison with the so-called linear economy (where natural resources are extracted, transformed into capital and consumer goods, and eventually disposed of in landfill or disposal facilities) is often made. In this context, emphasis is placed on a variety of mechanisms that modify the flow of products and materials through the economy, and ultimately result in lower rates of natural resource extraction. Previous OECD work in this area highlights three main mechanisms (McCarthy, Dellink and Bibas, 2018[3]): closing resource loops (the diversion of waste from disposal and subsequent transformation into secondary raw materials), slowing resource loops or flows (the retention of products, and their constituent materials, in the economy for longer periods), and narrowing resource flows (generating additional economic value from a fixed amount of natural resources).

Circular modes of production, and the business models that underpin them, represent the key activities that could realise a transition to a more resource efficient and circular economy. There is no clear consensus on what is and is not a circular business model. However, one key aspect – the defining one in the context of this report – is their relative sparing use of natural resource inputs. This results not only from facility level improvements in material productivity, but also from more fundamental changes in production and consumption patterns. For example, instead of using natural resource inputs more efficiently, renewable energy generation and the secondary raw material production do not use them at all.

Circular modes of production, and the business models that underpin them, involve fundamentally different ways of producing and consuming goods and services. The production of raw materials from waste, the reuse, repair, or remanufacture of unwanted or damaged products, and the sharing of already existing products are just three examples. Not all of these activities are necessarily new, but many are emerging more broadly in response to technological developments, urbanisation, heightened supply risks, and evolving consumer preferences. For policy makers, these developments raise a number of questions. What are the different business models that are of most interest from a circular economy perspective? What is their scalability potential? What are the environmental outcomes that can be expected from them, and which of them would merit policy support for scale-up? And finally, what are the policy measures that can help accelerate the scale-up of the most desirable business models?

This report addresses these questions by drawing together insights from the existing literature on circular business models. Chapter 2 introduces a typology of five key circular business models and highlights some of their shared characteristics and drivers for adoption. Chapter 3 uses well known examples to provide insights into the current market penetration, and potential scalability, of each of the headline business models. Chapter 4 addresses the environmental impact that could result from the widespread emergence of circular business models. It draws mostly on research from the lifecycle assessment literature, but also highlights the importance of economic mechanisms. Chapter 5 then briefly sets out the policy measures that could be implemented in order to promote the more widespread adoption of circular business models.

Notes

1 This trend will be offset, to some extent, by various market mechanisms. Higher resource prices will trigger new exploration and the discovery of new reserves. They will also encourage resource saving technological change and, in some cases, substitution towards other relatively affordable materials.

References

McCarthy, A., R. Dellink and R. Bibas (2018), "The Macroeconomics of the Circular Economy Transition: A Critical Review of Modelling Approaches", *OECD Environment Working Papers*, No. 130, OECD Publishing, Paris, http://dx.doi.org/10.1787/af983f9a-en. [3]

OECD (2019), *Global Material Resources Outlook to 2060: Economic Drivers and Environmental Consequences*, OECD Publishing, Paris, https://dx.doi.org/10.1787/9789264307452-en. [2]

OECD (2012), *OECD Environmental Outlook to 2050: The Consequences of Inaction*, OECD Publishing, Paris, http://dx.doi.org/10.1787/9789264122246-en. [5]

UN (2017), "World Population Prospects: key findings and advance tables", https://esa.un.org/unpd/wpp/publications/Files/WPP2017_KeyFindings.pdf (accessed on 18 May 2018). [1]

UNEP (2017), "RESOURCE EFFICIENCY: POTENTIAL AND ECONOMIC IMPLICATIONS", http://www.resourcepanel.org/sites/default/files/documents/document/media/resource_efficiency_report_march_2017_web_res.pdf (accessed on 23 April 2018). [4]

Chapter 2. Circular business models

This chapter focusses on circular business models, their key characteristics, and the main drivers for adoption. It begins by presenting a typology of the five headline circular business models that are discussed in this report: circular supply, resource recovery, product life extension, sharing, and product service system models. The key characteristics of each of these are then discussed, with a particular focus on the underlying business case. The chapter concludes with an overview of the higher level factors that could drive the adoption of circular business models in the longer term. Technological change and a range of emerging business risks are identified as being of particular importance.

This chapter identifies five key business models that could facilitate a transition towards a more resource efficient and circular economy. In this report, the term business model is used to describe how a firm creates, captures, and delivers value. In other words, it is a firm's competitive strategy. Osterwalder, Pigneur and Tucci (2010[1]) differentiate nine main elements of a business model. These are, the value proposition involved, who the key supply chain partners are, what resources and activities are involved in product creation, what their cost structure is, how products are delivered, which customer segments are targeted, how customer relationships are managed, and how revenues are collected. In this chapter, this framework is applied to five headline circular business models. Much of the focus is on character of the business case for an adopting firm, but attention is also given to the activities involved in production and the characteristics of revenue collection. Circular business models are often quite innovative in these respects.

Circular business models have a number of other distinguishing characteristics beyond their relatively sparing use of natural resource inputs. First, the underlying sales strategy tends to place less emphasis on maximising the sales volume of low-margin and short-lived products. Instead, the focus tends to be on selling higher quality products or, increasingly, marketing access to, rather than ownership of products. Second, the business case often leverages the value contained in already existing materials, components, and products. For example, by largely avoiding the use of new material and energy inputs, firms offering repair, refurbishment, or remanufacturing services can market products at a significantly lower cost than their traditional counterparts. Third, circular business models often involve greater levels of collaboration between different actors in the supply chain. There are often repeated interactions between suppliers and customers, and this can foster a heightened sense of customer loyalty. For example, operating within an industrial symbiosis framework requires significant inter-firm cooperation to ensure the ongoing availability of high quality of raw material inputs.

2.1. A typology of circular business models

The literature on circular business models is growing rapidly and contains a variety of different typologies. There are considerable differences in the level of granularity, as well as the classification approach that is taken. Some authors take a value chain perspective that structures business models into circular design, optimal use, and value recovery types (Achterberg, Hinfelaar and Bocken, 2016[2]). Others distinguish business models according to the material flows they address. IMSA (2015[3]) focus on short loops, long loops, cascades, and pure cycles while Lewandowski (2016[4]) focus on regeneration, sharing, optimisation, or looping. The activities implicit in all of these typologies overlap significantly, but are often given different names.

The typology that is adopted in this report draws on that developed by Accenture (Lacy and Rutqvist, 2015[5]). In contrast to the typologies discussed above, circular activities are categorised according to a business-centric perspective. This draws attention to the business proposition underlying each of the business models, which is significant given that widespread adoption will remain largely theoretical unless the private sector perceives substantial value. The five types of headline circular business models addressed in this report are: (i) circular supply models, (ii) resource recovery models, (iii) product life extension models, (iv) sharing models, and (v) product service system models (Table 2.1).

Table 2.1. Circular business models addressed in this report

	Circular supply	Resource recovery	Product life extension	Sharing	Product service system
Key characteristic	Replace traditional material inputs with renewable, bio-based, recovered ones	Produce secondary raw materials from waste	Extend product lives	Increase utilisation of existing products and assets	Provision of services rather than products. Product ownership remains with supplier
Resource efficiency driver	Close material loops	Close material loops	Slow material loops	Narrow resource flows	Narrow resource flows
Business model sub-types	Cradle to cradle	Industrial symbiosis	Classic long life	Co-ownership	Product-oriented
		Recycling	Direct reuse	Co-access	User-oriented
		Upcycling	Repair		Result-oriented
		Downcycling	Refurbishment		
			Remanufacture		
Main sectors currently applied in	Diverse consumer product sectors	Metals	Automotive	Short term lodging	Transport
		Paper and pulp	Heavy machinery	Transport	Chemicals
		Plastics	Electronics	Machinery	Energy
				Consumer products	

Note: The "sharing platform models" of Accenture have been renamed "sharing models" in order to avoid confusion with other business activities that utilise online platforms but that are not necessarily circular (see Box 2.2 for additional information).

While the distinction between each type of business model is clear in theory, it may be less so in practice. In some cases, firms adopt combinations of business models rather than one in isolation. For example, the adoption of product service system model – and the retention of product ownership that goes with it – may well serve to incentivise the parallel adoption of the product life extension model (Thompson et al., 2010[6]). In other cases, the decision to adopt a particular circular business model by a firm or group of firms can facilitate the adoption of a related business model by others. The adoption of the circular supply model, where strategic sourcing and design decisions are made early in a product's life, can improve the business case for component and material recovery further downstream.

Not all of the business models discussed included in this typology are necessarily new or novel. The resource recovery business model, where secondary raw materials are produced from waste, has operated in the metals sector for millennia. Similarly, ensuring that products attain their intended service life through reuse and repair has probably been widespread since the emergence of manufacturing. Other business models often appear to be novel, but have instead evolved from well-established traditional activities. One example involves peer to peer sharing of existing, but under-utilised, consumer assets. Sharing has always taken place; the distinction today is that it often takes place between individuals who did not previously know each other. In this case, it is the emergence and diffusion of digital networks, portable devices, and smart software systems that has enabled business model evolution.

Some circular business models do not have obvious historic equivalents. One example concerns circular supply models, where traditional material inputs are replaced by bio-based, renewable, or recoverable materials. These are probably emerging partly in response to greener consumer preferences in certain segments of the population. Firms are leveraging an increased willingness to pay for green products by ensuring that the environmental footprint of their supply chains is relatively small. Another example concerns product service system models in the context of dematerialised consumer products like e-books, streamed music and films, and digital newspaper subscriptions. Digitalisation has meant that the suppliers of these products can avoid the material input costs associated with producing physical products, and thereby produce additional output with virtually no additional cost.

Figure 2.1. The impact of circular business models on the linear economy

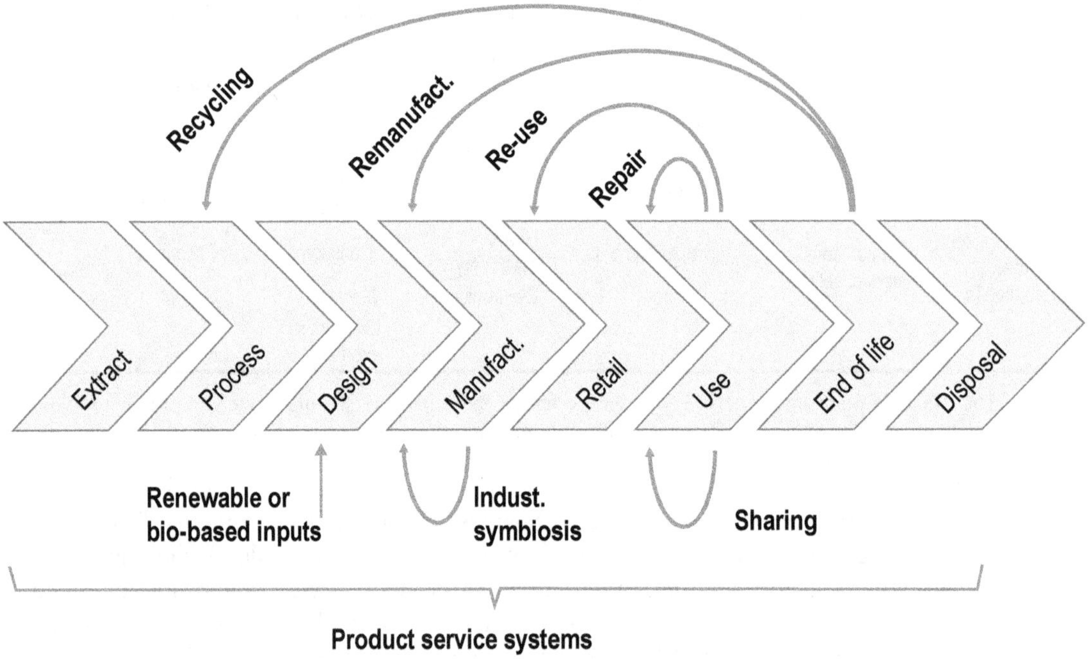

2.2. Individual circular business model characteristics

2.2.1. Circular supply models

Circular supply business models involve the replacement of traditional production inputs with bio-based, renewable, or recovered materials. By making strategic sourcing decisions at the outset of product development, adopting firms can reduce the environmental pressures emanating from their supply chains, while ensuring that the materials embedded in their products do not eventually become waste. In this sense, the circular supply model can be viewed as a form of resource recovery model, albeit one where material recovery is considered at a much earlier stage of the product lifecycle. Essentially, waste is designed away.

The philosophy underlying the circular supply model is often referred to as “cradle to cradle” product design.[1] This is intended to create a distinction with cradle to grave material flows, where the materials embedded in products end their lives in incineration or landfill facilities. Instead, these materials become inputs in the manufacture of new products. In this context, a parallel is often drawn with natural systems, where the death of an organism results in the cycling of nutrients to other organisms. Cradle-to-cradle is now also an official certification system, with around 500 certified products. One example of a firm selling C2C certified products is Tarkett, a global manufacturer of floor coverings (see Annex 1). Other examples include Advance Nonwoven, a Danish manufacturer of insulation material, and Green Packaging, an American manufacturer of food packaging.

The business case underlying the adoption of circular supply business models is twofold. First, replacing traditional inputs with bio-based, renewable, or recovered equivalents allows firms to market their products as "green". By differentiating their products in this way, adopting firms can target environmentally conscious consumers who are perhaps prepared to pay a premium for the knowledge that their consumption decisions have a smaller environmental footprint. Second, switching towards alternative material inputs is a way of managing regulatory and supply chain risk. With respect to the former, the introduction of more stringent environmental regulation is a possibility in many countries, and represents an important business risk for firms using polluting inputs in their production process. With respect to the latter, the natural resources from which key production inputs are derived are often geographically concentrated in a small number of countries, sometimes in politically unstable parts of the world. Manufacturers can at least partially mitigate the associated sourcing risk by integrating locally derived secondary materials into their supply chains.

Implementing the circular supply business model has implications for various aspects of a firm's operations. It influences the conceptualisation of the product design and the manufacturing process, and also concerns product branding and eventual distribution channels. Successful implementation requires that certain conditions are met. First, there must be sufficient market demand, and willingness to pay, for green products. This condition is likely to differ across jurisdictions; consumers in developing countries may have a limited ability to pay for products that are relatively expensive. Second, the bio-based, renewable, or recovered material inputs that are adopted must be good substitutes for the traditional materials that they replace. They also need to be sufficiently available and affordable; firms are unlikely to adopt the circular supply business model where it significantly increases their cost of doing business or risk profile.

2.2.2. Resource recovery models

Resource recovery business models involve the production of secondary raw materials from waste streams. There are three main activities involved, each of which is typically undertaken by different market actors (Gaillochet and Chalmin, 2009[7]). As its name suggests, *collection* involves the collection of the waste materials generated by households, businesses, and industry; it is generally organised by local governments. *Sorting* involves separation of a particular waste stream into its constituent materials; in some cases it is undertaken in public facilities and in others by the private sector. *Secondary production* involves the transformation of sorted waste material back into finished raw materials; it is generally undertaken by firms operating in the private sector. The resulting secondary raw materials – metals, plastics, paper, etc – are then sold to various manufacturing firms.

The business case underlying resource recovery models centres on the valorisation of the materials contained in waste streams. Raw waste is available at little or no cost; indeed the households and firms that generate it are often willing to pay to have it taken away. At the same time, finished secondary raw materials fetch significant prices on commodity markets. The challenge for firms adopting the resource recovery model is in ensuring that the unit cost of undertaking this valorisation process is sufficiently small relative to the market price of finished materials.

Adoption of the resource recovery business model is only likely under certain conditions. First, there needs to be a market for secondary raw materials. Concerns about the quality or composition of these materials mean that this is not always the case. Some technologically advanced sectors (aerospace for example) tend to avoid recovered materials because of uncertainty about their performance characteristics in extreme conditions. Similarly, food packaging providers in some countries are unable to use recovered plastics and paper due to hazardous chemicals regulation. Second, adoption of the business model requires that a sufficient volume of waste material being generated. This is not always the case, especially in regions characterised by low population densities or low levels of consumption. Although the transport of waste to central processing facilities is technically possible, it is not always economically feasible given the bulky and low value character of many waste streams.

The resource recovery business model, or recycling as it is better known, has several variants, each of which is described below:

Downcycling

Like recycling, downcycling involves the transformation of waste into secondary raw materials. The key difference is that the recovered materials are of an inferior quality, and can only be used as an input in a limited subset of applications. For example, in the context of paper and cardboard recycling, each additional loop results in a reduction of the length of cellulose fibres. As a result, recovered paper cannot always be used for the same applications that virgin paper can.

Upcycling

Upcycling is the opposite of downcycling. It involves the transformation of waste into secondary raw materials, and their subsequent use in relatively high value applications. An illustrative example is undertaken by Freitag, a German apparel manufacturer, that produces bags made from truck tarps, car seat belts, and bicycle inner tubes (see Annex 1).

Industrial symbiosis

Industrial symbiosis, or closed loop recycling as it is sometimes called, involves the use of production by-products from one firm as production inputs by another (Achterberg, Hinfelaar and Bocken, 2016[2]). Relative to classical recycling, there is more of an emphasis on commercial and industrial waste streams and, at the same time, fewer intermediate actors involved in material transformation. Industrial symbiosis is most common in industries that produce very pure and homogeneous material flows, such as the chemical industry. Some of these tight relationships develop organically. Most often, however, they are the result of carefully planned industrial parks that connect one firm with another via pipelines or short-distance truck deliveries (Taranic, Behrens and Topi, 2016[8]).

2.2.3. Product life extension models

As their name suggests, product life extension models involve extending the life of products. This is desirable from a circular economy perspective because products, and the materials embedded in them, remain in the economy for longer, and thereby potentially reduce the extraction of new resources. There are three mechanisms involved. First, manufacturers can extend the service life of their products by designing them in a way that increases durability. This is referred to as the classic long life model in the remainder of this report. Second, reuse and repair activities, and their associated business models, ensure that products actually attain their intended service life (rather than being prematurely discarded). Third, remanufacturing extends the life of products by "resetting the clock" – remanufactured products attain an entirely new service life. Each of these business model sub-types is summarised in Table 2.2 and discussed briefly below.

Table 2.2. Overview of product life extension models

	Key characteristic	Business case
Classic long life	The expected life of a product is extended through changes in product design	Manufacturers can charge a premium for higher quality, more durable products
Direct reuse	Involves the redistribution and reuse of products that would have otherwise been discarded before reaching their expected end of life	Firms that facilitate transactions of second-hand goods (whether online platforms or physical shops) can charge a percentage of the selling price
Maintenance and repair	By fixing or replacing defective components, maintenance and repair allows degraded products to reach their full expected life.	For original equipment manufacturers, extending product care beyond the point of sale may help to promote customer loyalty. In addition, repairing existing products can be a profitable activity for third party repair firms.
Refurbishment and remanufacturing	Gives products a "new life" by restoring them to their original working condition	Refurbished or remanufactured products are sold at a lower price than new ones, but may generate higher profit margins due to material cost savings

With the exception of the classic long life model, it is not necessarily the case that product life extension models are undertaken by the original equipment manufacturer (OEM). In many cases, it is actually third party operators that facilitate the reuse of second-hand goods, or carry out repair, refurbishment, or remanufacturing activities. The business case varies accordingly. For third party adopters, offering repair, refurbishment, or remanufacturing services is about leveraging the cost savings associated with using already existing materials and products as inputs. These activities produce products of a similar quality to new equivalents, but at a considerably lower cost. For original equipment manufacturers, the decision to adopt life extension activities probably rests upon two additional considerations. First, adoption is a strategic way of addressing the threat from third party firms and may foster greater customer loyalty (Long et al., 2017[9]). Second, in the case of remanufacturing, adoption can partially mitigate procurement risks associated with key material inputs.

Classic long life

As discussed above, the classic long life model involves designing products with longer service lives. The business case for adoption is similar to that for circular supply models; firms that produce higher quality products have an ability to charge customers higher prices. Essentially, low sales volumes are offset by a premium pricing strategy.

Direct reuse

In many cases, products are not disposed of because they have reached the end of their (functional) life, but because consumers decide to replace them with updated versions. For example, Cooper (2004[10]) finds that around one third of appliances in the UK are still in working order when thrown away. The direct reuse business model takes advantage of this by facilitating the redistribution of used products to new owners. In this way, products that would have otherwise been disposed of continue to remain in circulation.

Direct reuse is not usually facilitated by the original manufacturer, but by a third-party who distributes goods that already exist in the economy. In this context, internet reselling platforms such as *eBay* and *Craigslist* have gradually tapped into the market and are competing with more traditional second-hand shops and bulletin boards (Lacy and Rutqvist, 2015[5]). Because profit is usually made via a small margin of the reselling price, the residual value of the product should be high enough for reselling. It is, therefore, important that the product is not severely damaged and generally in good condition. A challenging aspect of this model is to reach a critical mass of sellers/donors and buyers to make the platform attractive.

Maintenance and repair

By fixing or replacing defective components, product maintenance and repair ensures that products reach their full expected service life. In this way, degraded products that would otherwise have been discarded of and replaced continue to remain in circulation. This is no small issue; research undertaken by WRAP (2011[11]) finds that 23% of the electronic equipment discarded in the UK could be reused or resold with minor or moderate repair. Fairphone, a smartphone manufacturer, is one example of a firm attempting to address this issue. By incorporating greater modularity into the design of their smartphones, Fairphone facilitates the repair of existing products and reduces demand for new equivalents.

Maintenance and repair is carried out by both original equipment manufacturers (such as Fairphone) and by third party firms (such as iMend or Mister Minit). For original manufacturers, a major benefit of integrating service components to the value proposition of a physical product is the high-quality branding and customer trust that it affords. Selling the same product at a price premium is also conceivable from a marketing point of view. Through potential multiple points of contact between the seller and buyer after the initial sale, there is furthermore a chance to build up higher brand loyalty, especially when customer experience has been positive (Bocken et al., 2016[12]).

Refurbishment and remanufacturing

Refurbishment and remanufacturing involve the restoration of degraded products, either for a fee, or for subsequent resale to original or new owners. In refurbishment, the emphasis is largely on aesthetic improvements, with limited restoration of product functionality (Spelman and Sheerman, 2014[13]). Remanufacturing, by contrast, is a broader concept that involves the restoration of used products to their original level of functionality (Box 2.1). As such, despite the usually lower sales price, remanufactured products are usually labelled “as good as new” (Parker et al., 2015[14]). Remanufacturing is usually carried out by the original equipment manufacturer (OEM), which has the both the technical expertise and the appropriate components to allow product performance to be fully restored.

Box 2.1. The definition of remanufacturing used in this report

According to the European Remanufacturing Network (Parker et al., 2015[14]), the only definition for remanufacturing that is recognised as a national standard is that produced by the British Standards Institution. BS 8887-2 states that remanufacturing involves "returning a product to at least its original performance with a warranty that is equivalent or better than that of new, newly manufactured product". Supplementary notes to this definition state that remanufacturing involves the dismantling of products, restoring and replacing components, and testing individual parts and the whole product to ensure it fits within the original design specifications. It is this process that ensures that remanufactured products have at least the same performance level as the original new product.

Remanufacturing can be a profitable business model; it has been adopted by an increasing number of multinationals worldwide. Its earning model is based upon generating additional revenue by reselling the same or similar products multiple times. Moreover, cost savings can be achieved by reducing the amount of virgin material and components being sourced. Often, a remanufactured product is 40% less expensive than a newly manufactured one (Le Moigne and Georgeault, 2016[15]). In times of highly volatile natural resource prices, this may lead to a reduced sourcing risk. The successful and profitable integration of an in-house remanufacturing capacity requires several factors to be in place, such as dedicated factory facilities, a specialized workforce, and a sophisticated reverse logistics system. Although remanufactured goods are usually cheaper than newly manufactured ones, they often come with a comparable quality standard and warranty which makes them an interesting alternative for customers. Products suited for the remanufacturing model are mostly capital intensive and durable. They should have long product life cycles and a modular design for easy disassembly and repair in order to be economically viable. Annex 1 provides a case example for heavy machinery manufacturer Caterpillar.

2.2.4. Sharing models

Sharing models, or sharing economy or sharing platform models as they are sometimes called, involve using under-utilised consumer assets more intensively, either through lending or pooling (Box 2.2). There are a variety of products that sit unused for much of their effective life; housing, vehicles, clothing, and tools are some examples. Research by the Ellen McArthur Foundation finds that the average European vehicle is parked 92% of the time and that, even when it is in use, only 1.5 of the available 5 seats are typically used (Ellen McArthur Foundation, 2015[16]). Sharing of these products has always taken place, but has become more widespread in recent years as the phenomenon of "sharing between strangers" has emerged. This has largely resulted from the emergence of various technologies – the internet, mobile phone technology, and the development of referral and reputational systems – that have reduced the transaction costs and risks associated with sharing assets.

Most of today's sharing practices are facilitated by online platforms, some of which – Airbnb for example – have become powerful market actors. Sharing models have two sub-types: *co-ownership and co-access*. The underlying business case for both is clear. Online platforms facilitate transactions between the owners of under-utilised assets and individuals seeking to use them; platform owners can generate a small margin on each related transaction. Significantly, because the capital cost of the underlying goods has already been paid (by owners), the up-front investment cost required to launch an online platform is significantly smaller than that required to become a traditional provider. Platforms usually also have very small operational costs and significant potential for scale up.

For the owners of under-utilised assets and products, the emergence of online platforms provides an opportunity to earn additional income. Unused apartments, rooms, vehicles, vehicle seats, clothing, or tools can be leveraged, rather than sitting idle. Potential buyers also benefit to the extent that shared products are cheaper than their traditional equivalents. For example, one reason why accommodation sharing has performed so strongly in recent years is because it is often available at a price discount to traditional hotel rooms. Several recent assessments find that the average price of an Airbnb listing was between 15% and 20% lower than a traditional hotel equivalent (STR, 2017[17]; Statista, 2017[18]).

Box 2.2. The definition of sharing models used in this report

There are widely diverging views about what activities sharing models encompass. This is partially a consequence of the use of the key enabling technology – online platforms – in a number of other closely related business models. The definition of sharing models used in this report follows that developed by Frenken and Schor (2017[19]), who describe the activities involved as "consumers granting each other temporary access to under-utilized physical assets, possibly for money". In this view, sharing models have three key aspects:

- They involve peer to peer or, alternatively, consumer to consumer (C2C) transactions. Transactions that involve renting or leasing products from firms are separate since, in many cases, they would considered as product service system business models (consider urban car sharing schemes such as Autolib or the leasing of idle industrial capacity for example).
- They involve the temporary, rather than permanent transfer of product ownership. Online platforms that facilitate the sale and purchase of second hand goods would be considered to fall under product life extension business models (consider EBay for example).
- They involve the more efficient use of under-utilised physical assets, rather than services provided by private individuals. Online platforms that facilitate the service transactions between individuals are examples of on-demand business models (consider Uber or Task Rabbit).

Focusing on the business activities facilitated by online platforms, rather than the platforms themselves, has two main advantages. First, not all of the business activities that utilise online platforms necessarily have the potential to improve material efficiency or stimulate a transition to a more circular economy. Consider the migration of traditional retail sales to online platforms such as Amazon or the emergence of on-demand services platforms such as Uber for example. Second, the regulatory issues relating to online platforms differ considerably according to the specific business activities involved. Consider the distinction between B2C and C2C transactions and questions about who is, and is not, considered to be a producer for tax (and other) purposes.

Co-ownership

The co-ownership variant of sharing models involves the lending of physical goods. The sharing of household tools and appliances on platforms like *Peerby* is one such example. Products that are especially suited for the co-ownership model are capital intensive, infrequently used, and have a low ownership rate (IDDRI, 2014[20]). Moreover, they must be easy to transport and should be durable, in order to allow for the increased usage during their effective lifespan. Urban areas are particularly suited to co-ownership models; high population densities reduce the transaction costs associated with a temporary change in product ownership (IDDRI, 2014[20]). Annex 1 provides examples of several sharing models.

Co-access

The co-access variant of sharing models involves allowing others to take part in an activity that would have taken place anyway. Thus, carpooling allows seats that would otherwise have remained empty to be occupied during a particular journey. *Blablacar* is a prominent example of this business model. Though its online platform, it links drivers intending to undertake long journeys with passengers that are willing to pay for a spare seat.

2.2.5. Product service systems models

Product service system (PSS) models combine a physical product with a service component. There are several variations, some of which place more emphasis on the physical product, and others that focus more on the service aspect. The typology used in this report follows that developed by Tukker (2004[21]). It separates product service system models into three main variants: product-oriented, user-oriented, and result-oriented PSS models. Each of these is briefly discussed below.

Product-oriented product service system models

Product-oriented PSS systems are focused mostly on the product end of the PSS spectrum. Manufacturing firms that adopt this business model continue to produce and sell products in a conventional way, but include additional after-sales service in the value proposition. Services may, for instance, take the form of maintenance contracts and repair offerings through extended product warranties or take back agreements (COWI, 2008[22]). For example, the high-end outdoor clothing company *Patagonia* guarantees to repair broken apparel and operates a platform for customers to sell their products as second-hand products.

User-oriented product service system models

User-oriented (or access-oriented as they are sometimes called) PSS models put products and services on a more balanced footing. Customers pay for temporary access to a particular product, typically through a short- or long-term lease agreement, while the service provider retains full ownership of the product. Urban car sharing schemes, office equipment leases, and garment rental services are widely cited examples of user-oriented PSS models. Another rapidly emerging example concerns the digitalisation of various forms of traditional media.[2] Online platforms like Amazon, Netflix, Spotify, and Coursera allow literature, film, music, and education to be consumed without ownership of the underlying books, CDs, DVDs etc.

User-oriented PSS models provide access to the services associated with a particular good without ownership of the good itself. That means that consumers only pay for a product when they actually need it; the upfront and ongoing costs of ownership are largely avoided.[3] In the case of urban car sharing schemes, customers can temporarily use a vehicle without having to bear the associated running, maintenance, and parking costs. In addition, user-oriented PSS models can also provide consumers with access to high quality or technologically advanced products that they could not otherwise afford. One example concerns clothing; it is common for individuals to lease, rather than own, some types of expensive garments.

Adopting a user-oriented PSS models can create various opportunities for firms. By retaining ownership of products, and the components and materials embedded in them, manufacturers can potentially mitigate a range of supply chain risks (access to, and price volatility of, material inputs for example). This is likely to be an important driver of business model adoption in certain situations (such as where the security of supply of key manufacturing inputs is uncertain), but not in others (such as where the business model is adopted by third party, non-manufacturing firms). In the latter case, the adoption of user-oriented PSS is probably motivated by a different set of opportunities. For example, for expensive goods such as vehicles and high-end clothing, there may be value in targeting consumers who are unable or unwilling to purchase new products, but who may be interested in paying for temporary access to them. Similarly, providing goods like literature and music digitally can reduce unit production costs while also increasing revenues (through the ability to sell advertising on the associated online platform).

Result-oriented product service system models

Result-oriented PSS models are situated at the service end of the PSS spectrum. Instead of marketing manufactured assets or goods in a traditional way, adopting firms market the services or outcomes provided by these goods. For example, an adopting firm might sell a heating outcome (maintaining a certain temperature level within a building), rather than the underlying heating equipment or energy inputs. Alternatively, an adopting firm may undertake the manufacturing of a particular brand's products rather than selling the capital equipment itself.[4] Essentially, contracts between suppliers and customers therefore describe a specific outcome, without necessarily specifying the means through which it is achieved (COWI, 2008[22]). This creates strong incentives for the efficient use of variable (and potentially polluting) inputs such as energy or chemicals. Result-oriented PSS models have been adopted in a range of sectors; US EPA (2017[23])gives the following three examples:

Energy service companies (ESCOs) offer energy efficiency and related services to their customers by assuming full performance risk for the project and products used. The level of compensation is tied closely to the energy efficiency savings they are able to accomplish. An example is the Dutch lighting company Philips which introduced 'Circular Lighting' or 'pay-per-lux' back in 2009. A client may agree with Philips on a specific level of brightness for a facility measured in lux. The task of Philips then is to provide the level of brightness with the most cost-effective lighting equipment possible (see additional details on this in annex 1).

Chemical management services (CMS) or chemical leasing aims at supplying and managing the customer's chemicals. The business model emerged first in the late 1980s in the US and has resulted in many long-term contract relationships (OECD, 2017[24]). Similar to the case of ESCO's, the compensation of the provider is linked to the quantity and quality of the service and not, as in traditional models, to the volume of the chemicals used. By taking full responsibility of the chemicals used, the providing firm will also be responsible for their handling at the end-of-life and have incentives to optimise these costs.

Integrated pest management (IPM) and *performance based pest management* (PPMS) is a special form of chemical leasing in the agricultural sector. The chemicals used for pest control are owned and handled by the providing company which possesses expertise about their optimal application. The compensation is not based on the chemical volumes sold, but on the level of crop loss prevented.

2.3. Drivers of circular business model adoption more generally

The business case for the adoption of circular business models is not static, but varies according to a broad set of societal level factors. Changes in consumer behaviour, the threat of new regulation, or concerns about the stability of key supply chains represent considerable business risks for firms operating traditional business models, and can stimulate switching towards greener, more circular modes of production. In a similar way, the appearance of new technologies can reduce the cost structure of relatively circular production, thereby creating opportunities for potential adopters. The following section presents a brief snapshot of the factors that are facilitating the adoption of circular business models.

2.3.1. Traditional "linear" modes of production: emerging business risks

Regulatory risk is becoming a significant concern for firms that operate traditional business models. One example concerns the emerging prospect of more widespread and stringent carbon pricing. This probably partly explains the broader adoption of internal shadow carbon pricing within the private sector (CDP, 2016[25]), and the diversification of some fossil fuel producers into renewable electricity technologies (Climate Home, 2016[26]). Another example concerns the potential introduction of more stringent product design and material recovery standards in various countries. The recent adoption of bans of certain products made from plastic (e.g. such as single carrier plastic bag bans) in a number of countries, as well as the recent European Union strategy on plastics are such examples (European Commission, 2018[27]), and probably represents a significant risk for firms whose products rely heavily on virgin plastic inputs.

Many emerging renewable energy and information communication technologies are heavily reliant on materials that are geographically concentrated in a handful of countries. More than 80% of the global production of rare earth elements – a key input in several renewable energy technologies – takes place in China (USGS, 2016[28]). Similarly, about half of global cobalt production – a key input in smartphone, laptop, and automotive batteries – takes place in the Democratic Republic of Congo. For the firms that manufacture these products, geo-politically related supply chain disruptions are an important operational risk, but one that can be partially mitigated by the adoption of the circular supply, resource recovery, or product service system models.

Heightened consumer awareness is creating new sources of reputational risk for established firms. Concerns about human rights abuses, dangerous working conditions, financing conflict have existed in the jewellery and clothing sectors for many years, and have led to a proliferation of labelling schemes intended to differentiate ethically produced products from otherwise. In the environmental sphere, similar concerns – about global warming, plastics pollution and biodiversity loss among others – may be creating new impetus for the adoption of greener or more circular modes of production. The recent pledges made by eleven leading consumer goods firms (including Coca Cola, Unilever, and L'Oréal) to use 100% reusable, recyclable, or compostable packaging by 2025 (Ellen McArthur Foundation, 2018[29]) may partially reflect this issue.[5]

2.3.2. Emerging technologies as a driver for the adoption of more circular modes of production

The appearance and diffusion of new technologies has also been an important factor in the evolution and growth of circular business models. The emergence of the internet and the widespread uptake of digital devices have been particularly important. First, increased connectivity has reduced the transaction costs and risk associated with sharing goods, and increased the convenience of leasing rather than owning goods. Second, connectivity has allowed, in combination with smart sensor technology, real time monitoring of product performance, which is probably facilitating certain types of product service system. Third, connectivity has allowed, in combination with digitalisation, a variety of consumer products to be significantly dematerialised. In addition to the content related goods described above, digitalisation has also affected education (though the growth of so-called massive open online courses) and work travel (through the emergence of teleconferencing).

Improvements in more traditional production technologies have also improved the business case for some circular business models. In the case of the circular supply model, the rapid improvements in solar and wind generation technologies are well documented, and have allowed renewable facilities to become increasingly competitive with their fossil fuel based equivalents. In the case of the resource recovery business model, the emergence of mechanised material sorting facilities (MRFs) has significantly improved the separation of different waste streams, thereby reducing the cost of secondary material production. In the case of the repair and remanufacturing business models, improvements in sensor technology have allowed faults to be diagnosed relatively quickly, again improving the underlying business case.

Technological change is also creating a variety of risks in the context of resource use and environmental pressure. The emergence and diffusion of a variety of labour saving technologies – ranging from robotics in production to snow movers and leaf blowers in consumption – may have actually increased the environmental footprint of some activities. In addition, rebound effects, which are discussed further in Section 4.4, have probably offset at least some of the reductions in resource extraction that have been realised by efficiency improvements. Finally, the continued growth of green technologies may be shifting the environmental burden associated with resource extraction and use away from the atmosphere (in the form greenhouse gas and sulphur and nitrogen oxide emissions for example) towards water and land. The extraction and processing of the aluminium, copper, lithium, and rare earth elements used widely in the automotive, energy, and ICT sectors has a variety of often toxic by-products such as mine waste, process tailings, and smelter residues.

Notes

1 Circular supply models are also often said to facilitate an economy that is "regenerative by design".

2 This is perhaps an example of a hybrid circular business model. In many cases, it involves short-term access to, rather than ownership of, goods and services; a key characteristic of result-based PSS models (e.g. Spotify or Netflix). In other cases, it is no more than a traditional sales model, but with transactions of digital rather than physical products (e.g., e-books or digital newspaper subscriptions).

3 That said, ownership of electronic devices is normally required for consumers to participate in these product offerings (Netflix and Spotify for example).

4 MakeTime, a United States based online platform, facilitates the procurement of precision manufactured parts by connecting product assemblers (the client) with upstream production facilities (the supplier).

5 Coca Cola has also pledged to, (i) collect and recycle the same volume of packaging that it produces, and (ii) incorporate 50% recycled content into new packaging (both by 2030) (Coca Cola, 2018[144]).

References

Achterberg, E., J. Hinfelaar and N. Bocken (2016), *The Value Hill Business Model Tool: identifying gaps and opportunities in a circular network*, http://www.scienceandtheenergychallenge.nl/sites/default/files/multimedia/organization/sec/2016-06-16_NWO_Sc4CE/NWO%20Sc4CE%20-%20Workshop%20Business%20Models%20-%20Paper%20on%20Circular%20Business%20Models.pdf (accessed on 13 September 2018). [2]

Bocken, N. et al. (2016), "Product design and business model strategies for a circular economy", *Journal of Industrial and Production Engineering*, Vol. 33/5, pp. 308-320, http://dx.doi.org/10.1080/21681015.2016.1172124. [12]

CDP (2016), *Embedding a carbon price into business strategy*, https://b8f65cb373b1b7b15feb-c70d8ead6ced550b4d987d7c03fcdd1d.ssl.cf3.rackcdn.com/cms/reports/documents/000/001/132/original/CDP_Carbon_Price_report_2016.pdf?1474899276 (accessed on 13 September 2018). [25]

Climate Home (2016), *Exxon, Shell, Total, Statoil renew clean energy drive*, http://www.climatechangenews.com/2016/05/23/exxon-shell-total-and-statoil-make-clean-energy-plays/ (accessed on 13 September 2018). [26]

Cooper, T. (2004), "Inadequate Life?Evidence of Consumer Attitudes to Product Obsolescence", *Journal of Consumer Policy*, Vol. 27/4, pp. 421-449, http://dx.doi.org/10.1007/s10603-004-2284-6. [10]

COWI (2008), *Promoting Innovative Business Models with Environmental Benefits*, http://www.cowi.com (accessed on 13 September 2018). [22]

Ellen McArthur Foundation (2018), *Eleven companies take major step towards a New Plastics Economy*, https://www.ellenmacarthurfoundation.org/news/11-companies-take-major-step-towards-a-new-plastics-economy (accessed on 13 September 2018). [29]

Ellen McArthur Foundation (2015), *GROWTH WITHIN: A CIRCULAR ECONOMY VISION FOR A COMPETITIVE EUROPE*, https://www.ellenmacarthurfoundation.org/assets/downloads/publications/EllenMacArthurFoundation_Growth-Within_July15.pdf (accessed on 13 September 2018). [16]

European Commission (2018), *Plastic Waste: a European strategy to protect the planet, defend our citizens and empower our industries*, http://europa.eu/rapid/press-release_IP-18-5_en.htm (accessed on 18 January 2018). [27]

Frenken, K. and J. Schor (2017), "Putting the sharing economy into perspective", *Environmental Innovation and Societal Transitions*, Vol. 23, pp. 3-10, http://dx.doi.org/10.1016/J.EIST.2017.01.003. [19]

Gaillochet, C. and P. Chalmin (2009), *From waste to ressources : world waste survey 2009*, https://www.researchgate.net/publication/41222409_From_waste_to_ressources_world_waste_survey_2009 (accessed on 13 September 2018). [7]

IDDRI (2014), *The sharing economy: make it sustainable*, http://www.iddri.org (accessed on 13 September 2018). [20]

IMSA (2015), *Circular business models: an introduction to IMSA's circular business model scan*, https://groenomstilling.erhvervsstyrelsen.dk/sites/default/files/media/imsa_circular_business_models_-_april_2015_-_part_1.pdf (accessed on 13 September 2018). [3]

Lacy, P. and J. Rutqvist (2015), *Waste to wealth : the circular economy advantage.* [5]

Le Moigne, R. and L. Georgeault (2016), "Remanufacturing: Une Formidable Opportunité Pour La France Industrielle de Demain", https://www.wmaker.net/eco-circulaire/attachment/656994/ (accessed on 13 September 2018). [15]

Lewandowski, M. (2016), "Designing the Business Models for Circular Economy—Towards the Conceptual Framework", *Sustainability*, Vol. 8/1, p. 43, http://dx.doi.org/10.3390/su8010043. [4]

Long, X. et al. (2017), "Strategy Analysis of Recycling and Remanufacturing by Remanufacturers in Closed-Loop Supply Chain", *Sustainability*, Vol. 9/10, pp. 1-29, https://ideas.repec.org/a/gam/jsusta/v9y2017i10p1818-d114402.html (accessed on 13 September 2018). [9]

OECD (2017), *Economic Features of Chemical Leasing*, https://one.oecd.org/document/ENV/JM/MONO(2017)10/en/pdf (accessed on 13 September 2018). [24]

Osterwalder, A., Y. Pigneur and C. Tucci (2010), *Clarifying Business Models: Origins, Present, and Future of the Concept*, https://www.researchgate.net/publication/37426694_Clarifying_Business_Models_Origins_Present_and_Future_of_the_Concept (accessed on 13 September 2018). [1]

Parker, D. et al. (2015), *Remanufacturing Market Study*, http://www.remanufacturing.eu/assets/pdfs/remanufacturing-market-study.pdf (accessed on 13 September 2018). [14]

Spelman, C. and B. Sheerman (2014), *Triple Win: The Social, Economic, and Environmental Case for Remanufacturing*, http://www.policyconnect.org.uk/apmg (accessed on 13 September 2018). [13]

Statista (2017), *Airbnb - Statistics & Facts*, https://www.statista.com/topics/2273/airbnb/ (accessed on 13 September 2018). [18]

STR (2017), *Airbnb & Hotel Performance*, http://www.str.com/Media/Default/Research/STR_AirbnbHotelPerformance.pdf (accessed on 13 September 2018). [17]

Taranic, I., A. Behrens and C. Topi (2016), *Understanding the Circular Economy in Europe, from Resource Efficiency to Sharing Platforms: The CEPS Framework*, http://www.ceps.eu (accessed on 13 September 2018). [8]

Thompson, A. et al. (2010), *Benefits of a Product Service System Approach for Long-life Products: The Case of Light Tubes*, http://www.ep.liu.se/ecp/077/011/ecp10077011.pdf (accessed on 13 September 2018). [6]

Tukker, A. (2004), “Eight types of product–service system: eight ways to sustainability? Experiences from SusProNet”, *Business Strategy and the Environment*, Vol. 13/4, pp. 246-260, http://dx.doi.org/10.1002/bse.414. [21]

US EPA (2017), “U.S. EPA Sustainable Materials Management Program Strategic Plan”, https://www.epa.gov/sites/production/files/2016-03/documents/smm_strategic_plan_october_2015.pdf (accessed on 23 April 2018). [23]

USGS (2016), *USGS Minerals Information: Commodity Statistics and Information*, https://minerals.usgs.gov/minerals/pubs/commodity/ (accessed on 18 May 2018). [28]

WRAP (2011), *Realising the Reuse Value of Household WEEE*, http://www.wrap.org.uk (accessed on 13 September 2018). [11]

Chapter 3. The current scale and potential scalability of circular business models

This chapter moves from describing different circular business models to assessing their potential scalability. Each of the headline business models considered in this report is analysed in terms of, i) their current market share, and ii) their ability to significantly scale up. The former draws upon existing market data from a variety of sources, while the latter is based on a review of the literature relating to these business models. The chapter concludes by summarising the current market penetration of circular business models, and by identifying several fundamental barriers to their future adoption.

3.1. Introduction

This chapter moves from describing different circular business models to assessing their potential scalability. Scalability is important. Achieving a genuine transition to a more circular economy – with significant decoupling of economic growth from natural resource extraction and use – will be unlikely if circular business models continue to occupy small economic niches in a limited number of countries.

Most of the circular business models identified in Chapter 2 are not new. The resource recovery and product life extension business models have existed in the form of recycling, re-use, and repair for many millennia. As will be shown in this chapter, these activities are relatively mature in most sectors; the key question is therefore what kinds of technological, policy, or behavioural change could stimulate more widespread adoption. Other circular business models are emerging rapidly in response to one or more underlying drivers. In the case of the circular supplies business model, increased environmental awareness along with a higher willingness to pay for green products seem to have been important. In the case of sharing business models, the availability of the internet, and the development of referral and reputational systems, have been key drivers. For these business models, the key questions are, (i) whether continued scale up is feasible once significant market share is attained, and (ii) whether they are potentially applicable to sectors other than those currently involved (e.g., how much potential do sharing models have beyond the accommodation sector?).

The current scale, and potential scalability, of individual business models and business model sub-types will vary according to the economic sector considered. Potential scalability of a particular business model will also vary according to the extent that related business models have already emerged. In some cases, this will involve synergies. The adoption of PSS business models will tend to provide manufacturers with incentives to design more modular and recyclable products, with clear benefits for material recovery activities further downstream. In other cases, there will be trade-offs; widespread investment in material recovery facilities may increase demand for secondary raw materials to the point where product repair or remanufacturing becomes less attractive. Assessing the scalability of all business models in all sectors, and the interactions between them, is beyond the scope of this work. This chapter aims to provide insights through the use of four key examples: recycling in the metals sector, product remanufacturing, sharing in short term accommodation sector, and product service systems in the transport sector.

Predicting the market penetration of a particular business model beyond the immediate future is a necessarily subjective exercise. Business model adoption will be driven by the attractiveness of the underlying business case which, in turn, will depend on the evolution of an array of technological, policy, and behavioural factors. The approach taken in this chapter is to document current rates of market penetration and then, on the basis of the respective business model characteristics and the existence of any fundamental barriers to scale up, develop a view of potential future scalability.

3.2. Resource recovery business models: the example of metal recycling

3.2.1. Current market penetration

Secondary metal production – producing finished metal products from recycled scrap – accounts for around 15% to 30% of the global production of the most widely used metals:

steel, aluminium, copper (Figure 3.1). This figure has fluctuated over the last 50 years, but with a notable recent decline for steel and aluminium, and an equally notable increase for copper. For less common, but nonetheless strategically important metals such as lithium and the group of rare earth elements, secondary production accounts for a negligible share of total output (UNEP, 2013[1]). Although this situation may be slowly changing with the recent increase in demand for these materials, there remains little data available. Given the low market share of secondary metal producers, there seems to be considerable potential for the scale up of the resource recovery business model in the metal sector. A similar conclusion could probably be drawn for other recyclable commodities with similarly limited market shares (plastics and paper for example).

Figure 3.1. Evolution of secondary market share for finished steel, aluminium, and copper

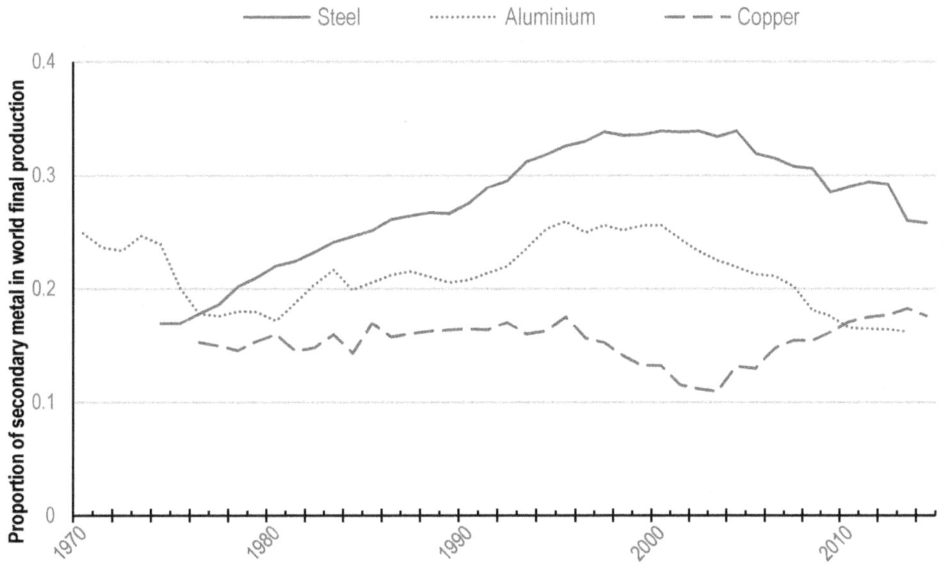

Source: USGS (2016[2]), *Minerals Information Commodity Statistics*, https://on.doi.gov/2OyIuAU; World Steel (2016[3]), *World Steel Association Statistics*, https://bit.ly/2pg71Qj; ABREEE (2016[4]), *Resources and Energy Statistics*, https://bit.ly/2D6vuBp

3.2.2. Future scalability

One fundamental constraint on the scalability of the resource recovery business model is the limited availability of scrap feedstock at a given point in time. In contrast to the primary metal production, where additional demand can be reliably met through the exploitation of known ore reserves, the amount of scrap available for processing each year is constrained, both by the decommissioning of long lived capital goods (e.g. buildings and vehicles), and by the disposal of short lived consumer goods (e.g. food packaging). In practice, this means that, even if recycling rates for a particular metal did approach 100%, it is unlikely that secondary production could satisfy more than half of total metal demand in the foreseeable future. This issue is currently most relevant for steel, where global recycling rates are thought to be around 80% (UNEP, 2013[1]), while the proportion of secondary output in total production is only around 25% (Figure 3.1).[1]

For the vast majority of other metals, recycling rates are typically lower than 25% (UNEP, 2013[1]), and it is a lack of economic competitiveness that currently holds back the resource recovery business model. Producing finished metal products from recycled scrap is not cost competitive with doing so from virgin mineral ores. There are a number of underlying reasons for this, ranging from the labour intensity of product disassembly, sorting, and recycling on the supply side, to concerns about the performance of secondary materials in high performance applications on the demand side. Market failures and policy misalignments are also important; one example of the latter concerns the government support that is provided to extractive and processing industries in a number of countries (OECD, 2017[5]). These issues hold back the development of well-functioning and liquid secondary materials markets, and this in itself has negative implications for secondary competitiveness (both by hindering the realisation of scale economies in production, and by contributing to the relatively high price volatility (Figure 3.2) that restricts investment in secondary production capacity.

Figure 3.2. Price volatility in the iron ore and steel scrap markets: 2010 to 2016

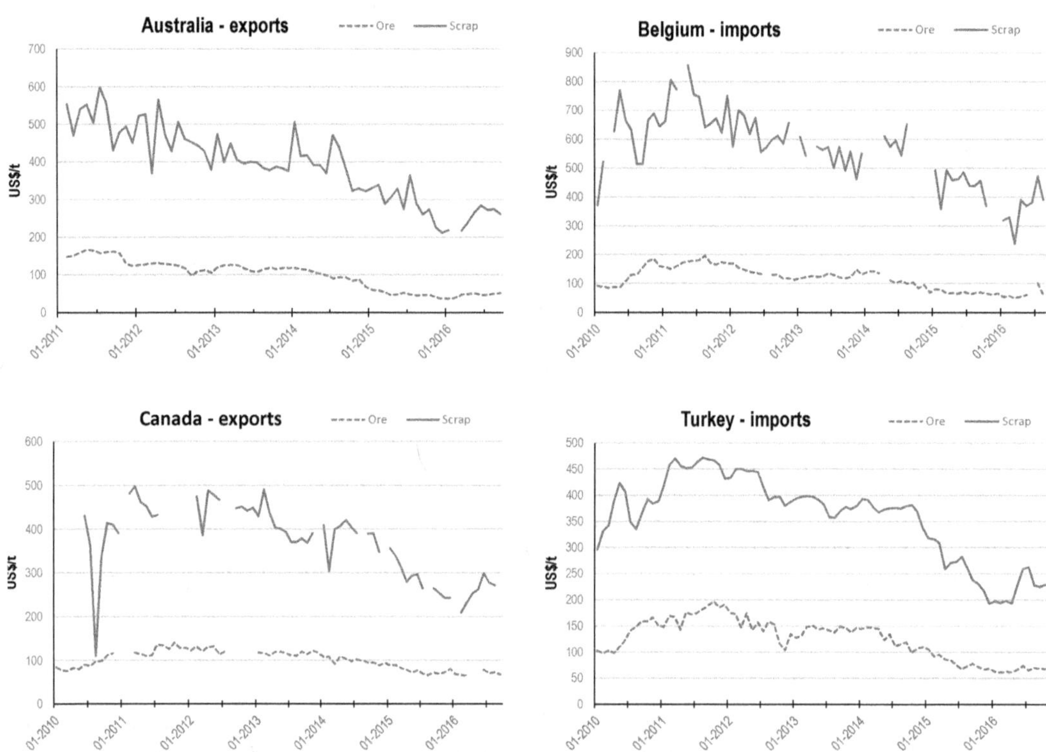

Note: Not all data points are available for Canada, Belgium and Australia.
Source: UN COMTRADE (2018[6]), *International Trade Statistics Database,* https://bit.ly/2jL1FIk

3.3. Product life extension models: the example of remanufacturing

3.3.1. Current market penetration

The global market for remanufactured goods is thought to be worth around €100 billion (Le Moigne and Georgeault, 2016[7]; AmCham, 2017[8]). Data from the United States International Trade Commission indicate that the United States was the world's largest remanufacturing economy in 2011, with around USD 43 billion in remanufactured output

(US ITC, 2012[9]). Production data is also available for the European Union (Parker et al., 2015[10]) and China (Wang, 2016[11]), which in 2015 produced EUR 30 billion and CNY 150 billion (EUR 20 billion) of remanufactured goods respectively.

Remanufacturing remains relatively small in terms of its share of total manufacturing. In both the EU and the US, remanufacturing generally accounts for no more than 4% of the output from any given sector (Table 3.1 and Table 3.2). One exception involves the European aerospace industry, where remanufacturing apparently represents 11% of total sectoral output. Part of the reason for this appears to be that general repair services have been lumped to together with remanufacturing.[2] More generally, it is apparent from the US and EU data that remanufacturing is better established in some sectors – aerospace, heavy duty and off-road equipment, medical equipment, and tyres – than in others – consumer products, EEE, and IT products. This is consistent with more anecdotal evidence regarding remanufacturing; the examples that are frequently cited include Caterpillar (heavy duty and off-road equipment), Siemens (medical imaging equipment), and Michelin (tyres).

Table 3.1. US remanufacturing statistics - 2011

	Production (USD m)	Employment	Market share (%)
Aerospace	13,046	35,200	2.6
Automotive parts	3,212	30,700	1.1
Consumer products	659	7,600	0.1
HDOR equipment	7,771	20,800	3.8
IT products	2,682	15,400	0.4
Machinery	5,795	26,800	1
Medical devices	1,463	4,100	0.5
Retreaded tyres	1,399	4,900	2.9
All other	3,974	23,000	1.3
Wholesalers	-	10,900	
Total	*40,001*	*179,400*	

Source: Parker et al. (2015[10]), *Remanufacturing market study,* https://bit.ly/2NiylMi

Table 3.2. EU remanufacturing statistics - 2011

	Production (EUR m)	Firms	Employment	Market share (%)
Aerospace	12,400	1000	71,000	11.5
Automotive parts	7,400	2363	43,000	1.1
EEE	3,100	2502	28,000	1.1
Furniture	300	147	4,000	0.4
HDOR equipment	4,100	581	31,000	2.9
Machinery	1,000	513	6,000	0.7
Marine	100	7	1,000	0.3
Medical devices	1,000	60	7,000	2.8
Rail	300	30	3,000	1.1
Total	*29,700*	*7203*	*194,000*	

Source: Parker et al. (2015[10]), *Remanufacturing market study,* https://bit.ly/2NiylMi

3.3.2. Future scalability

Given the low share of remanufacturing in total manufacturing output, there appears to remain considerable potential for future scale up. Although there is limited data available, remanufactured output does seem to have grown in recent years. In the US, for instance, remanufacturing expanded at 7% annually between 2009 and 2011 (US ITC, 2012[9]). Projections for the EU suggest that remanufactured output could double or triple during the next decade, perhaps employing as many as 600 000 workers by 2030 (Parker et al., 2015[10]). Achieving these projections will require that a number of important barriers to the further development of remanufacturing be addressed.

There does not appear to be any inherent characteristic of remanufacturing that might limit its future growth. Achieving significantly higher rates of market penetration will instead depend on the attractiveness of the underlying business case. Although there are a number of assessments that highlight the theoretical profitability of remanufacturing (Lavery et al., 2013[12]),[3] it is clear that it continues to be largely uneconomic under current market conditions. Two key costs that are often highlighted are those related to labour inputs and the transport of used cores. With respect to the former, it is generally accepted that remanufacturing, because it cannot be automated to the same extent as traditional manufacturing, is relatively labour intensive. While this is positive from a job creation perspective, the additional costs involved also represent a barrier to market penetration. With respect to core transport, it has been noted that restrictions on cross border flows of used and second-hand products can make it difficult for remanufacturing firms to regain access to their products.

More broadly, it is possible that many traditional manufacturers may be unwilling to adopt remanufacturing, even when external calculations seem to indicate that it makes economic sense. There are at least three reasons.

- There may be concerns about product cannibalisation (Agrawal, Atasu and van Ittersum, 2015[13]). Many traditional manufacturing firms market a suite of products within a given product category, often ranging from entry level versions with limited functionality to high end versions with more functionality. It may be that sales of remanufactured products – necessarily priced at levels below those of premium products – displace sales of traditionally manufactured premium products, thereby reducing overall profits.
- Manufacturers may be unable to capture all of the value associated with designing products that are amenable to remanufacturing (those that are relatively modular and easily disassembled). For example, the entry of low-cost third party repair, refurbishment, and remanufacturing firms can mean that end of use products do not find their way back to the original equipment manufacturer. This lack of certainty reduces the attractiveness of adopting remanufacturing.
- Although remanufacturing produces products that are "as good as new", it does not necessarily follow that consumers are willing to pay "new", or even "near-new" prices for them. In some cases, this is because the performance of the remanufactured product is not as good as that for a contemporary version of the same product, even if it is as good as that for the original version. In other cases, prices are probably lower because consumers are unprepared to pay for a product that is perceived as being as old or out of fashion. This may be a partial

explanation for why remanufacturing appears to be less common in consumer goods sectors (personal electronics for example) than in B2B applications.

3.4. Sharing models: the example of short-term lodging

3.4.1. Current market penetration

Airbnb is perhaps the best known platform for marketing short term lodging. It was founded in 2008 and has experienced exponential growth since.[4] By November 2016, Airbnb had around 1 million individual listings, giving it roughly the same capacity as the largest traditional hotel providers (STR, 2017[14]).[5] This growth can be largely attributed to the price competiveness of Airbnb relative to traditional providers. According to several recent assessments, the average price of an Airbnb listing was between 15% and 20% lower than a traditional hotel equivalent (STR, 2017[14]; Statista, 2017[15]). Figure 3.3 shows the growth in annual Airbnb guest arrivals (or individual bookings – regardless of their length) between 2008 and 2016.

Although Airbnb's growth has been dramatic, its relative share of overall bookings remains small. Recent analysis indicates that it only accounts for 1-6% of short stays in a cross section of ten major North American and European cities (STR, 2017[14]). Similarly, CBRE Hotels estimates that Airbnb hosts in New York generated $450 million in revenue for the year ended September 2015, only around 5% of the $9 billion in lodging revenue generated in the city that year (Travel Weekly, 2016[16]). Given these figures, there appears to be clear potential for the continued scale up of sharing models in the short-term lodging sector.

Figure 3.3. Airbnb guest arrivals: 2008 – 2015

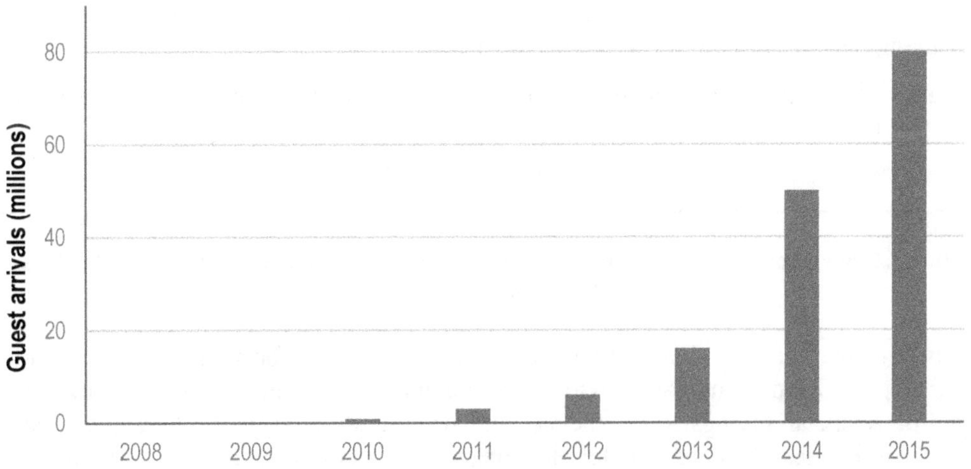

Source: Recode (2017[17]), *Airbnb is on track to rack up more than 100 million stays this year*, https://bit.ly/2uBH9Cj

3.4.2. Future scalability

The increased consumer choice and price reductions that are facilitated by sharing models will tend to encourage their continued growth, both within the short term lodging sector and elsewhere. That said, the availability of spare capacity and the introduction of additional regulatory restrictions represent barriers that could curtail scale up.

In most cases, shortages of spare capacity are probably of limited relevance since there will always be a proportion of individuals unwilling to lease their assets. Similarly, and particularly with respect to short term lodgement, it seems likely that there will always be a proportion of travellers who prefer the relative familiarity of traditional hotels. Preferences for traditional forms of consumption[6] also tend to be reinforced by the transaction costs that are associated with participating in sharing business models. Sharing of existing assets introduces a variety of time costs – the search for an appropriate product, contacting the owner to arrange pick-up times, pick-up and return of the shared good – that can collectively render sharing less attractive unattractive. Importantly, both of these issues are likely to be partly mitigated if sharing models continue to emerge. Trust in platforms like Airbnb tends to increase as they become more widespread, and this may result in individuals becoming more willing to share their assets.[7] Similarly, the transaction costs associated with asset sharing are likely to decrease as more people take part; increased participation increases the likelihood that an available asset is located nearby. These effects highlight the catalytic nature of sharing models, a feature that partly explains their rapid recent growth.

Regulatory restrictions could represent a more significant barrier to the scale up of sharing models (Box 3.1). For example, in the context of short term lodging, a number of city authorities (in London, Amsterdam, and San Francisco among others) have placed a cap on the maximum number of nights that an Airbnb host can offer each year (AirBnb, 2018[18]). Authorities in other cities have imposed other restrictions. For example, in 2015, city authorities in San Francisco made it illegal for hosts to offer short term leases for residences other than their primary address (San Francisco Business Portal, 2018[19]). Similarly, authorities in New York have made short term (less than 30 days) sub-lets of any type illegal unless the owner of the residence is living there during the time of the lease (The Herald, 2017[20]). Although it is unclear how city rules will evolve in the future, it seems likely that any continued increase in stringency will affect the scale up of sharing models in the short term lodging segment.

Figure 3.4 shows the reduction in Airbnb's year-on-year revenue growth in New York since 2011.

Box 3.1. Social concerns and the growth of sharing and other platform based business models

The recent emergence of sharing (e.g., AirBnb) and other platform based business models (e.g., Uber and Amazon) has provided consumers with a number of clear benefits (in terms of financial savings, convenience, and product diversity). At the same time, the emergence of these business models has triggered concerns about lost profitability and jobs in traditional service activities, foregone government tax revenues, and increasing housing prices and rents.

The diversity of these business models, the speed at which they have emerged, and uncertainty about their costs and benefits has led to a fragmented policy response. Some governments have taken a relatively "hands off" approach while others have intervened more strongly (see the above examples relating to AirBnb for example).

At the centre of the debate lie concerns about consumer protection and, relatedly, fair competition. Should "peer producers" of goods and services be regulated in the same way as traditional providers? Or do the reputational and referral systems embedded in most online platforms render certain forms of traditional regulation no longer fit for purpose? To what extent should the incomes accruing to "peer producers" be subject to taxation – are there thresholds below which the administrative costs become excessive? The answers to these questions are far from clear, but there is a significant body of ongoing research that will help to provide new insights. Interested readers may refer to the ongoing OECD's Going Digital project and, more specifically, the work streams on online platforms in the context of taxation (OECD, 2017[21]), regulation (OECD, 2018[22]), and consumer protection (OECD, 2016[23]).

Figure 3.4. Airbnb revenue growth in New York City: 2011 – 2017

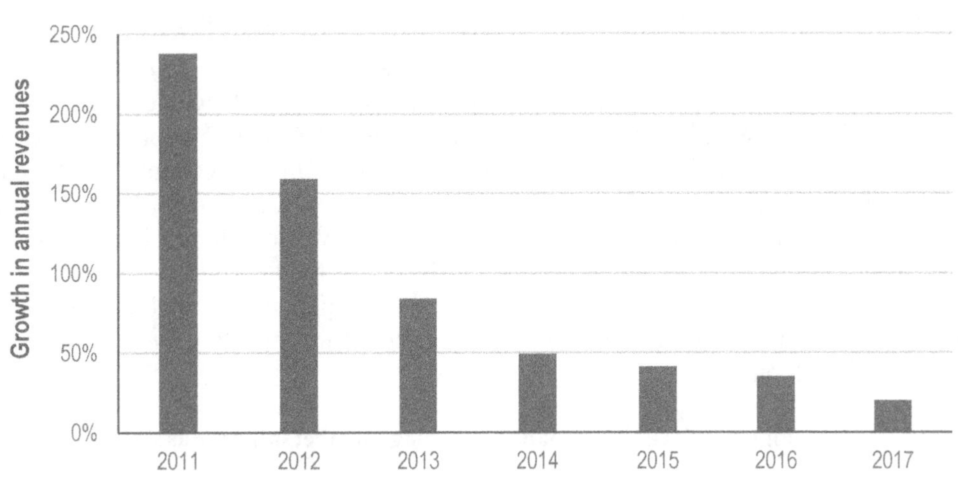

Source: Statista (2017[15]), *Airbnb – Statistics and Facts,* https://bit.ly/2D8LqDc

Although sharing models are currently most visible in the short term lodging segment, it is also relevant in other sectors. Analysis undertaken for France indicates that sharable goods – those characterised by high upfront costs and infrequent use – account for about 25% of household expenditure (IDDRI, 2014[24]). The major product categories that are highlighted include vehicles, clothing, furniture, household appliances, and tools. Although there is little data available, and perhaps with the exception of vehicles, the practice of sharing these goods via online platforms is probably less widespread than it is for short term lodging. Clearly, the behavioural barriers highlighted above for lodging – the willingness of asset owners and leasers to participate in sharing – are relevant. Transaction costs may also be particularly important, especially for bulky goods like furniture which are difficult to transport even locally.

3.5. Product service systems: the example of user oriented product service systems – mobility

3.5.1. Current market penetration

Urban bike and car sharing schemes are examples of user oriented product service systems. The underlying business model involves business to consumer (B2C) transactions and should not be confused with the consumer to consumer (C2C) transactions associated with car-pooling (e.g., BlaBlaCar) or bike (e.g., Peerby) or car sharing (e.g., Getaround). These mobility schemes are also distinct to traditional rental operations. First, rental locations are not limited to fixed locations such as airports, railway stations, and shops. Instead, bikes and vehicles can be accessed throughout urban areas with the use of GPS based mobile applications. Second, pricing schemes and typical usage patterns differ. Urban bike and car sharing schemes generally charge users an up-front membership fee along with a variable fee based on the time (often minutes or hours) that the bike or vehicle is used for. Users have strong incentives to restrict usage to short periods, which partially explains why this type of sharing is primarily an urban phenomenon. The following discussion focusses on urban car sharing schemes. Currently operating examples include Zipcar (privately owned and operated enterprise operating in the United States) and Autolib (government owned enterprise operating in Paris).

Urban car sharing schemes have grown rapidly recent years (Figure 3.5). Between 2006 and 2014, the global fleet of shared vehicles grew from 11 500 vehicles to 104 000 vehicles while membership grew from 350 000 people to 4 800 000 people (Shaheen and Cohen, 2016[25]). That said, as of 2014, the fleet of shared vehicles accounted for less than 0.1% of the almost 1 billion strong global in-use car fleet (OICA, 2015[26]). According to the same publication, the biggest markets for carsharing worldwide are Europe (46% of global members and 56% of global carsharing fleet) and North America (34% of global members and 23% of global fleet). In sum, the market penetration of B2C car sharing schemes remains very low in cities in developed countries, and largely non-existent in cities in the developing world.

Figure 3.5. Global urban car sharing membership trends

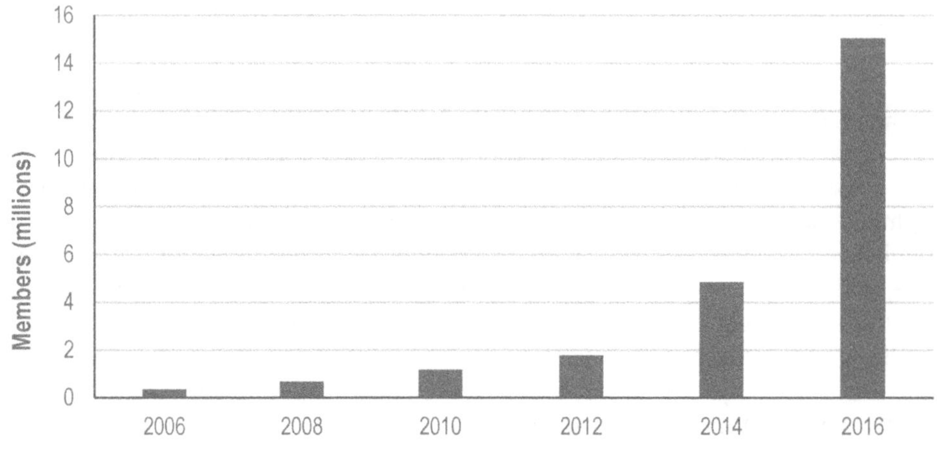

Source: Shaheen and Cohen (2016[25]), *Innovative Mobility Car Sharing Outlook*, https://bit.ly/2NMMUXZ

3.5.2. Future scalability

There are no inherent characteristics of urban car sharing schemes that will obviously hinder their continued emergence.[8] To the extent that the mobility provided by such schemes is comparable to that provided by alternative transport modes, both in terms of convenience and affordability, car sharing will probably continue to emerge and capture higher rates of market share. Projections developed by Navigant Research (2015[27]) indicate that global car sharing membership could reach 23 million people by 2024, a fivefold increased relative to today. The same projections suggest that much of the future growth will be seen in Asia, where car sharing has not developed to the same extent as in Europe and North America. At present, Asia, Africa, and Latin America comprise over 78% of the world's population, but only account for 20% of the car sharing market (WRI, 2015[28]). Car sharing could help to prevent or delay the uptake of private car ownership of the growing middle-class in these regions.

The future uptake of urban car sharing schemes will mostly depend on consumer acceptance of the concept, as well as the profitability of the underlying business model. With respect to the former, one potential barrier relates to the availability of parking space in public areas. The convenience of urban car sharing schemes is greatly diminished when it is difficult to find parking at the conclusion of the use period. Another barrier related to consumer acceptance is the value that individuals often appear to attach to vehicle ownership *in itself*. Private vehicles provide a mobility service – often one that is more convenient than shared vehicles – but they also seem to provide other sources of wellbeing. In particular, part of what individuals may be paying for when buying a vehicle is the status that comes with ownership. This is one explanation for why, despite providing much the same mobility service, there is a large price differential between mid-range mass produced cars and high performance sports cars.[9] If vehicles are a status good or, in other words, if individuals buy them for reasons other than the mobility service they provide, then this may become a significant obstacle to the continued emergence of urban mobility schemes.

More generally, the suite of product service system business models – including product-oriented, user-oriented, and result-oriented varieties – appear to be applicable in just about any market involving the use of manufactured goods. As highlighted in Chapter 2, PSS models are already being applied in both B2B and B2C markets in sectors as diverse as apparel, aviation, chemicals, electronic appliances, energy, office furniture, and, of course, transport. They are also being applied increasingly in the context of digital products: e-books, streamed music, digital media, and online education for example.

Despite this broad applicability (which is a significant strength from a scalability perspective), it is clear that the uptake of PSS business models continues to be rare in most sectors. There are probably two main reasons:

- As emphasised by Tukker (2015[29]), B2C variants of PSS business models have historically been held back by a strong consumer desire for product ownership: "for consumers, having control over things, artefacts, and life itself is one of the most valued attributes". This point about ownership is essentially the same as the one made above in the context of urban car sharing schemes.
- It is not clear that PSS business models represent a better commercial strategy than traditional sales models. There probably are advantages in certain situations, such as where there is a considerable supply risk affecting manufacturing inputs, or where the adoption of the PSS model allows manufacturers to signal the

superior quality of their product. But more generally, some costs can be higher, especially if the PSS introduces new labour inputs, or when it involves more networked production systems with associated transaction costs (Tukker, 2015[29]). In addition, the management of ongoing client service relationships is unlikely to be within the core business expertise of manufacturing firms, a factor that also probably hinders adoption.

3.6. Conclusions

Circular business models occupy a peripheral position in most markets (Table 3.3). Recycled pulp and paper, metals, and plastics represent small proportions of global material output, while remanufactured industrial and consumer products represent an even smaller share of global manufacturing. Sharing of under-utilised housing capacity has grown rapidly, but now only accounts for several percent of the annual short stays in most major cities. The same is true for user-oriented product service system models, which account for less than 1% of the market that they are perhaps most well known in: urban mobility. One notable exception to the above pattern is the emergence of result-oriented PSS in the automotive market. European and North American vehicle manufacturers have widely outsourced the chemical coating phase of the production process on a price per-area basis (OECD, 2017[30]).

Although this chapter did not include an explicit focus on geographic differences, it is apparent that some circular business models are more successful in certain contexts than others. In most cases, market penetration seems to have been greatest in developed country settings. Circular supply models, for example, have been successful here, perhaps because of a greater consumer ability to pay for "green" products. Similarly, sharing models involving short term lodging and transport have experienced rapid growth in wealthier cities, probably because of the relative availability of under-utilised assets there. There are also some notable exceptions. One example relates to certain forms of product sharing and leasing, which are becoming more visible in developing countries. Bike sharing schemes are common in large Chinese cities; more than two million shared bikes are available in Beijing alone (BBC, 2017[31]). Another example concerns the resource recovery model. Trade data indicates that a significant portion of the material recovery value chain (specifically the reprocessing of sorted waste back into secondary raw materials) is located in developing countries (Eurostat, 2018[32]).

There remains considerable scope for the future growth of circular business models. However, any such growth will be subject to economic realities – more widespread adoption of these business models will not take place unless there is a solid underlying business case. In some cases, the attractiveness of the business case may diminish as market share increases. For example, in the context of recycling, it is well documented that the unit cost of recovering steel or aluminium from household appliances is significantly higher than recovering them from relatively simple bulky products like vehicle chassis'. In other cases, the attractiveness of the business case will improve as market share increases. This is especially relevant for those business models characterised by network effects; consumer acceptance of platform models and car sharing schemes is likely to increase as the membership base – and services offered – grows. It may also be relevant for other business models that are characterised by some form of path dependence or that benefit in some way from the emergence of related business models.[10] In the context of remanufacturing, addressing the trade rules that hinder cross border flows of product cores would allow remanufacturing to become more widespread and, perhaps, generate lower costs through either learning externalities or scale economies.[11]

Table 3.3. Summary of current market penetration of selected circular business models

	Sector	Market penetration	Explanation
Waste as value: recycling	Pulp and paper	38%	Of total global output
	Metals	0 - 30%	
	Plastics	13%	
Product life extension: refurbishment	Various	2 - 3%	Of EOL products
	Smartphones	4 - 8%	Of annual manufactures
Product life extension: remanufacturing	Aerospace	2 - 12%	Of total manufactures
	Machinery	3 - 4%	
	Automotive	1%	
	Consumer and EEE	0 - 1%	
Idle Capacity: co-access	Lodging	1% - 6%	Of total short term bookings
PSS: result-oriented (chemicals)	Automotive	50 - 80%	Of manufacturer uptake
	Aerospace	5 - 15%	
PSS: result oriented (digital content)	Music	50%	Of total industry revenues
	Books	25 - 35%	
PSS: result-oriented (lighting & heating)	Various	4 - 7.5%	Of potential ESCO uptake
PSS: user-oriented (car sharing)	Transport	<1%	Of total global car fleet

Source: Plastics and paper recycling data are from Geyer, Jambeck and Law (2017[33]) and in Van Ewijk, Stegemann and Ekins (2017[34]) respectively. Data for smartphone refurbishment is taken from analysis by Gartner, cited in Tech Crunch (2015[35]) and Trend Force (2017[36]). Data for refurbishment of other consumer products are from European Commission (2016[37]). Data for result-oriented PSS in the chemicals, literature and music, and lighting and heating sectors are taken from OECD (2017[30]), IFPI (2017) and the Guardian (2017[38]), and Stuart and Goldman (2014[39]).

As highlighted in Section 2.3, the business case for circular business models will also evolve alongside broader societal level trends. Changes in policy frameworks, consumer preferences, and available technologies have the potential to stimulate adoption in much the same way as in the past.[12] The emergence of technologies associated with the so-called Fourth Industrial Revolution seems particularly promising in the context of circular business models. Improvements in robotics, artificial intelligence, sensor technology, and 3D printing will have widespread consequences, particularly when coupled with increasingly pervasive digital networks. The Internet of Things (IoT), which is just one of the potential implications of these developments, will present an array of opportunities for more efficient food and energy use (Jagtap, 2017[40]; Ashman, 2017[41]). Research undertaken by the WEF (2016[42]) in New York city suggests that digital connectivity in concert with smart sensors could also vastly improve the convenience of ride sharing, to the extent that 80% of all journeys could be shared.

Based on the material presented in this chapter, it is also possible to highlight several more fundamental barriers that affect the scalability of each major business model:

- *Resource recovery models* may become constrained by feedstock shortages if recycling rates approach 100%. At present, this is probably only relevant in the steel market, where global recycling rates are thought to be around 80%. Even if there was a business case for recycling the final 20% of scrap contained in waste flows, it is unlikely that secondary steel production could meet more than half of global of global steel demand. This constraint may be eased in the long term as the materials contained in long lived capital goods and infrastructure are released into waste streams (assuming that future growth in demand for materials is sufficiently low).

- More widespread adoption of the *remanufacturing business model* appears to be hindered by manufacturers' concerns about cannabilisation of premium sales and the entry of third party remanufacturers. More generally, the limited market share held by the family of *product life extension models – reuse, repair, refurbishment, and remanufacture* – may be a result of a strong consumer desire for the "latest" product, an effect which is itself modulated by the rate of product innovation,. This is one explanation for why the *remanufacturing* business model has been more sucessful in a B2B than a B2C context.
- *Sharing models* have emerged rapidly in response to several technological and social innovations, and will probably continue to do so given the network effects that are inherent to these models. One obvious constraint to future growth is the availability of spare capacity, and the proportion of owners willing to make it available. Another issue concerns the longevity of current policy frameworks. In an effort to address equity and competitiveness concerns resulting from the growth of peer to peer sharing, policy makers in a number of cities have implemented new regulations (with respect to short term lodging for example) that may serve to slow scale up.
- *Product service system models* have been adopted across a diverse range of sectors, and have seen some success in applications like chemical leasing (OECD, 2017[30]). Barriers to scale up elsewhere vary significantly according to the sub-model considered (user-oriented vs result-oriented for example) and the sector it is applied in. Generally speaking, one major barrier, particularly in a B2C context, seems to have been consumers' desire for the convenience and other intangible benefits that come with product ownership. Another issue concerns the underlying business case for the adoption of PSS; it often seems to be far from clear.

Notes

1 Limits on the availability of scrap feedstock will be partially eased in the medium term as an increasingly large anthropogenic metal stock is decommissioned and replaced.

2 See page 57 of Parker et al. (2015[17]).

3 These assessments generally highlight the retention of product cores, and the associated avoided material input costs, as a key cost advantage relative to traditional manufacturing.

4 Airbnb turned its first profit in 2016, and was recently valued at around USD 30 billion (CNBC, 2017).

5 Airbnb actually had around 3 million listings in November 2016. However, many of them – unavailable, shared, and private rooms for example – are not obviously comparable to a traditional hotel booking. STR therefore excludes these from their analysis.

6 Individual product ownership in the case of durable goods, and traditional service providers (e.g., hotels) in the case of services.

7 There may also be a feedback mechanism from the growth of sharing platforms to the overall availability of spare capacity. For example, there is some anecdotal evidence that the emergence of Airbnb has led to investments in the housing stock that may not have taken place otherwise.

8 One issue relates to the feasibility of car sharing schemes in low density areas. The business case is probably greatly diminished in rural areas where a larger number of stations would be required to serve a given population. This barrier is probably minor given the high proportion of people living in urban areas.

9 To be sure, some of this differential probably also reflects differing performance levels.

10 For example, the adoption of product service system model – and the retention of product ownership that goes with it – may well serve to incentivise the parallel adoption of the product life extension model.

11 Path dependency may also be relevant for the resource recovery business model. Secondary material markets are characterised by high levels of price volatility, and this probably makes investment in secondary processing facilities less attractive. Addressing the barriers that hinder secondary material markets will boost output and thereby lead to more liquid markets with less price volatility.

12 Consider the role that waste management policies and new technologies have played in stimulating (respectively) higher recycling rates and the sharing of underutilised consumer assets.

References

ABREE (2016), *Resources and Energy Statistics*, https://industry.gov.au/Office-of-the-Chief-Economist/Publications/Pages/Resources-and-energy-statistics.aspx (accessed on 18 May 2018). [4]

Agrawal, V., A. Atasu and K. van Ittersum (2015), "Remanufacturing, Third-Party Competition, and Consumers' Perceived Value of New Products", *Management Science*, Vol. 61/1, pp. 60-72, http://dx.doi.org/10.1287/mnsc.2014.2099. [13]

AirBnb (2018), *Night Limits: Frequently Asked Questions*, https://www.airbnb.com/help/article/1628/night-limits--frequently-asked-questions (accessed on 13 September 2018). [18]

AmCham (2017), *China (Ningbo) Remanufacturing Industry International Cooperation Forum*, https://www.amcham-shanghai.org/en/article/china-ningbo-remanufacturing-industry-international-cooperation-forum-0?lang=en (accessed on 13 September 2018). [8]

Ashman (2017), *The Internet of Things: paving the way for renewable energy? – Capgemini Worldwide*, https://www.capgemini.com/2017/08/the-internet-of-things-paving-the-way-for-renewable-energy/ (accessed on 13 September 2018). [41]

BBC (2017), *Beijing bans new bikes as sharing schemes cause chaos - BBC News*, https://www.bbc.com/news/business-41197341 (accessed on 13 September 2018). [31]

European Commission (2016), *Study on socioeconomic impacts of increased reparability of increased reparability - EU Law and Publications*, https://publications.europa.eu/en/publication-detail/-/publication/c6865b39-2628-11e6-86d0-01aa75ed71a1 (accessed on 13 September 2018). [37]

Eurostat (2018), *Eurostat - Trade in recyclable raw materials*, http://ec.europa.eu/eurostat/tgm/table.do?tab=table&plugin=1&language=en&pcode=cei_srm020 (accessed on 28 March 2018). [32]

Geyer, R., J. Jambeck and K. Law (2017), "Production, use, and fate of all plastics ever made", *Science Advances*, Vol. 3/7, p. e1700782, http://dx.doi.org/10.1126/sciadv.1700782. [33]

IDDRI (2014), *The sharing economy: make it sustainable*, http://www.iddri.org (accessed on 13 September 2018). [24]

Jagtap, S. (2017), *IoT Concepts for Improving the Resource Efficiency of Food Supply Chains*, http://www.manufacturingfoodfutures.com/documents/utilization-of-internet-of-things-concepts-to-improve-resource-efficiency-of-food-supply-chains-sandeep-jagtap.pdf (accessed on 13 September 2018). [40]

Lavery, G. et al. (2013), *The Next Manufacturing Revolution*, http://www.2degreesnetwork.com (accessed on 13 September 2018). [12]

Le Moigne, R. and L. Georgeault (2016), "Remanufacturing: Une Formidable Opportunité Pour La France Industrielle de Demain", https://www.wmaker.net/eco-circulaire/attachment/656994/ (accessed on 13 September 2018). [7]

Navigant Research (2015), *Carsharing Programs*, https://www.navigantresearch.com/reports/carsharing-programs (accessed on 13 September 2018). [27]

OECD (2018), *ONLINE PLATFORMS: A PRACTICAL APPROACH TO THEIR ECONOMIC AND SOCIAL IMPACTS*, https://one.oecd.org/document/DSTI/CDEP(2018)5/en/pdf (accessed on 13 September 2018). [22]

OECD (2017), *Economic Features of Chemical Leasing*, https://one.oecd.org/document/ENV/JM/MONO(2017)10/en/pdf (accessed on 13 September 2018). [30]

OECD (2017), *MAPPING SUPPORT FOR PRIMARY AND SECONDARY METAL PRODUCTION*, https://one.oecd.org/document/ENV/EPOC/WPRPW(2016)2/FINAL/en/pdf (accessed on 13 September 2018). [5]

OECD (2017), *THE POSSIBLE ROLE OF DIGITAL PLATFORMS IN THE COLLECTION OF VAT/GST ON ONLINE SALES*, https://one.oecd.org/document/CTPA/CFA/WP9(2017)6/en/pdf (accessed on 13 September 2018). [21]

OECD (2016), *PROTECTING CONSUMERS IN PEER PLATFORM MARKETS: EXPLORING THE ISSUES*, https://one.oecd.org/document/DSTI/CP(2015)4/REV2/en/pdf (accessed on 13 September 2018). [23]

OICA (2015), *Vehicles in use*, http://www.oica.net/category/vehicles-in-use/ (accessed on 13 September 2018). [26]

Parker, D. et al. (2015), *Remanufacturing Market Study*, http://www.remanufacturing.eu/assets/pdfs/remanufacturing-market-study.pdf (accessed on 13 September 2018). [10]

Recode (2017), *Airbnb is on track to rack up more than 100 million stays this year — and that's only the beginning of its threat to the hotel industry - Recode*, https://www.recode.net/2017/7/19/15949782/airbnb-100-million-stays-2017-threat-business-hotel-industry (accessed on 28 August 2018). [17]

San Francisco Business Portal (2018), *Short-Term Rental*, https://businessportal.sfgov.org/start/starter-kits/short-term-rental (accessed on 13 September 2018). [19]

Shaheen, S. and A. Cohen (2016), *Innovative Mobility Carsharing Outlook*, https://cloudfront.escholarship.org/dist/prd/content/qt49j961wb/qt49j961wb.pdf?t=pa6fa3&v=lg (accessed on 13 September 2018). [25]

Statista (2017), *Airbnb - Statistics & Facts*, https://www.statista.com/topics/2273/airbnb/ (accessed on 13 September 2018). [15]

STR (2017), *Airbnb & Hotel Performance*, http://www.str.com/Media/Default/Research/STR_AirbnbHotelPerformance.pdf (accessed on 13 September 2018). [14]

Stuart, E., C. Goldman and D. Gilligan (2014), *The U.S. ESCO Industry: Recent Trends, Current Size and Remaining Market Potential*, http://aceee.org/files/proceedings/2014/data/papers/3-319.pdf (accessed on 13 September 2018). [39]

Tech Crunch (2015), *Upgrades Fueling Second Hand Smartphone Sales Boom, Says Gartner | TechCrunch*, https://techcrunch.com/2015/02/18/reuse-dont-recycle/?guccounter=1 (accessed on 13 September 2018). [35]

The Guardian (2017), *'Screen fatigue' sees UK ebook sales plunge 17% as readers return to print | Books | The Guardian*, https://www.theguardian.com/books/2017/apr/27/screen-fatigue-sees-uk-ebook-sales-plunge-17-as-readers-return-to-print (accessed on 13 September 2018). [38]

The Herald (2017), *Major blow for Airbnb users: New law to restrict New York City apartment rentals | Newcastle Herald*, https://www.theherald.com.au/story/4444330/major-blow-for-airbnb-users-new-law-to-restrict-new-york-city-apartment-rentals/?cs=34 (accessed on 13 September 2018). [20]

Travel Weekly (2016), *Airbnb vs. the hotel industry*, https://www.travelweekly.com/Danny-King/Airbnb-vs-hotel-industry (accessed on 13 September 2018). [16]

Trend Force (2017), *Global Smartphone Production Volume Totaled 1.36 Billion Units; Samsung Held On as Leader While OPPO and Vivo Burst into Global Top Five*, https://press.trendforce.com/node/view/2741.html (accessed on 13 September 2018). [36]

Tukker, A. (2015), "Product services for a resource-efficient and circular economy – a review", *Journal of Cleaner Production*, Vol. 97, pp. 76-91, http://dx.doi.org/10.1016/J.JCLEPRO.2013.11.049. [29]

UN Combrade (2018), *UN Comtrade | International Trade Statistics Database*, https://comtrade.un.org/ (accessed on 05 June 2018). [6]

UNEP (2013), *Metal Recycling – Opportunitites, Limits, Infrastructure (Full report)*, United Nations Environment Programme, http://www.resourcepanel.org/sites/default/files/documents/document/media/e-book_metals_report2b_recyclingopportunities_130919.pdf (accessed on 18 May 2018). [1]

US ITC (2012), *Remanufactured Goods: An Overview of the U.S. and Global Industries, Markets, and Trade*, http://www.usitc.gov (accessed on 13 September 2018). [9]

USGS (2016), *USGS Minerals Information: Commodity Statistics and Information*, https://minerals.usgs.gov/minerals/pubs/commodity/ (accessed on 18 May 2018). [2]

Van Ewijk, S., J. Stegemann and P. Ekins (2017), "Global Life Cycle Paper Flows, Recycling Metrics, and Material Efficiency", *Journal of Industrial Ecology*, http://dx.doi.org/10.1111/jiec.12613. [34]

Wang, Y. (2016), *Remanufacturing Mission to China*, https://connect.innovateuk.org/web/remanufacturing/article-view/-/blogs/new-remanufacturing-standards- (accessed on 13 September 2018). [11]

WEF (2016), *Understanding the Sharing Economy*, http://www3.weforum.org/docs/WEF_Understanding_the_Sharing_Economy_report_2016.pdf (accessed on 13 September 2018). [42]

World Steel (2016), *Crude Steel Production*, https://www.worldsteel.org/statistics/statistics-archive/steel-archive.html. . [3]

WRI (2015), *Carsharing: A Vehicle for Sustainable Mobility in Emerging Markets*, http://wrirosscities.org/sites/default/files/WRI_Carsharing_Vehicle_Sustainable_Mobility_Emerging_Markets.pdf (accessed on 13 September 2018). [28]

Chapter 4. The environmental impacts of circular business models

This chapter focuses on the environmental potential of circular business models. Drawing primarily on insights from the lifecycle assessment (LCA) literature, it assesses and compares the environmental footprint of goods and services produced via circular modes of production to those produced via more traditional means. Thus, recycled materials are compared to those made from virgin natural resources, remanufactured products are compared to new products, and the sharing or leasing of assets is compared to conventional ownership. While the environmental potential of circular business models is found to be broadly positive, the analysis also identifies several risks and unintended consequences that could result from their more widespread adoption.

4.1. Introduction

One reason for the recent interest in promoting a circular economy transition is the reduction in environmental impacts that could result. Circular business models, by closing resource loops and by slowing and narrowing resource flows, will, in theory, reduce the environmental footprint of production and consumption activities. That said, what is the evidence that these business models actually serve to displace resource extraction, processing, and disposal? And how does this translate into improved environmental outcomes? Which business models hold the greatest promise in this respect? These are the questions that this chapter attempts to address.

Establishing the environmental impacts associated with the emergence of circular business models is complex task for various reasons:

There are five business models considered in this paper, all of which have distinct sub-types. Each individual business model, or business model sub-type, operates in more than one economic sector. For example, sharing models are best known in the short term lodging and transport sectors, but are also relevant across a wider range of consumer products.[1] This diversity makes it difficult to generalize about the likely environmental impacts.

The emergence of a particular business model in a specific economic sector will have implications across a range of environmental impact categories including, but not limited to, global warming, particulate air pollution, acidification, eutrophication, toxicity, and solid waste generation potential.

Changes in each environmental impact category can emerge at different points in the product lifecycle. For example, remanufacturing heavy machinery probably reduces the greenhouse gas emissions associated with upstream material extraction, transport, and processing but, to the extent that it results in an energy efficiency differential between new and remanufactured products, it can also affect the emissions during the machinery's in-use phase.

The environmental impacts of a particular business model probably change as that business model emerges. For example, it is likely that the greenhouse gas mitigation potential associated with recycling will decrease at high recycling rates.

The emergence of a particular business model in a specific sector will lead to changes in relative prices and an array of indirect economic effects. The resulting changes in activity levels in other sectors will also have an environmental impact.

The intention in this chapter is to be as comprehensive as possible, however the above complexity serves to limit what can be feasibly covered.

The environmental impact associated with the emergence of a circular business model depends on both the market share that it captures (and the feedbacks this has on output from traditional modes of production, and on the wider economy) and on the relative environmental footprint of the circular and traditional modes of production. This chapter sets out to address both issues. Section 4.2 describes insights from intuitive approaches such as the circularity ladder concept. Section 4.3 draws on the life cycle analysis (LCA) literature to provide insights into the environmental footprint of different business models. The main weakness of these studies is their engineering approach; little attention is given to economic mechanisms and to the extent that circular modes of production will actually displace other activities. Section 4.4 therefore addresses economic effects, and particularly how the emergence of a particular circular business model might alter the structure of the broader economy.

4.2. Insights from the circularity ladder concept

The environmental desirability of different solid waste management options is embedded in the concept of a waste hierarchy (Box 4.1). In this framework, waste prevention is considered to be preferable to waste disposal because the environmental pressures associated with the mobilisation and disposal of materials are avoided. Different circular business models have different implications for the volume and ultimate destination of industrial and municipal solid wastes. Some business models – those relating to product life extension for example – probably serve to reduce the amount of waste generated. Others – resource recovery business models for example – are unlikely to influence waste generation, but will divert the waste that is generated away from disposal activities. Mapping the incidence of each circular business model to the waste hierarchy may therefore provide some insight into their relative environmental impacts.

Box 4.1. The waste hierarchy

The waste hierarchy is a concept that guides waste management policy in many OECD and non-OECD countries. Although the goal or objective of the waste hierarchy is rarely made explicit, it is often interpreted to be the minimization of the environmental impacts associated with the various solid waste management options (e.g. SEI, 2005 ([1])). Various versions of the hierarchy exist; the version embedded in the EU Waste Framework Directive (EU Directive 2008/98/EC) is perhaps the most cited. It ranks solid waste management options from most to least preferable as follows: (i) prevention, (ii) preparing for re-use, (iii) recycling, (iv) other recovery (e.g., energy), (v) disposal. In other words, from an environmental perspective, the priority should be to first limit the generation of waste, then to recycle and recover what is generated, and only then to dispose of what remains. This hierarchy is broadly consistent with the idea that the main objective of the circular economy is to maintain the value of products, components, and materials at their highest level.

This approach to assessing the relative environmental desirability of different circular business models has been undertaken by De Groene and Ethica (2015[2]), who term the resulting output the "circularity ladder" (Figure 4.1). Based on their work, product life extension and sharing models appear to be environmentally preferable to resource recovery business models. Product life extension and sharing business models, by slowing resource loops and narrowing resource flows respectively, have the potential to reduce the amount of waste generated. In contrast, the influence of resource recovery business models tends to be limited to diverting already existing waste towards material and energy recovery facilities. Product services can have an influence throughout the entire waste hierarchy. Product-oriented PSS variants, by including after sales service in the sales proposition, extend the life of products and prevent waste generation. Result-oriented PSS variants can have a similar impact since service providers have a greater incentive to use material inputs sparingly. Both result-oriented and user-oriented PSS variants, where product ownership is retained by the manufacturer, can create better incentives for recycling.

The circularity ladder approach provides a useful "first-pass" assessment of the relative environmental desirability of different circular business models. There are two main issues to be aware of. First, the waste hierarchy ranks waste management options according to the environmental impacts associated with the end of life phase of the product lifecycle; it is unclear whether the ranking remains valid when the entire product life-cycle is taken into account. For example, if the in-use environmental impacts of long-lived, energy intensive consumer products are considered, it may not always be the case that product repair is preferable to recycling, especially when new products have significant improve energy or water efficiency. Second, the circularity ladder provides little insight into the likely *magnitude* of the environmental benefits associated with different business models. Questions regarding the size of the potential greenhouse gas savings associated with remanufacturing activities, or the reduction in acidification potential associated with metal recycling, are better addressed by LCAs.

Figure 4.1. The circularity ladder concept

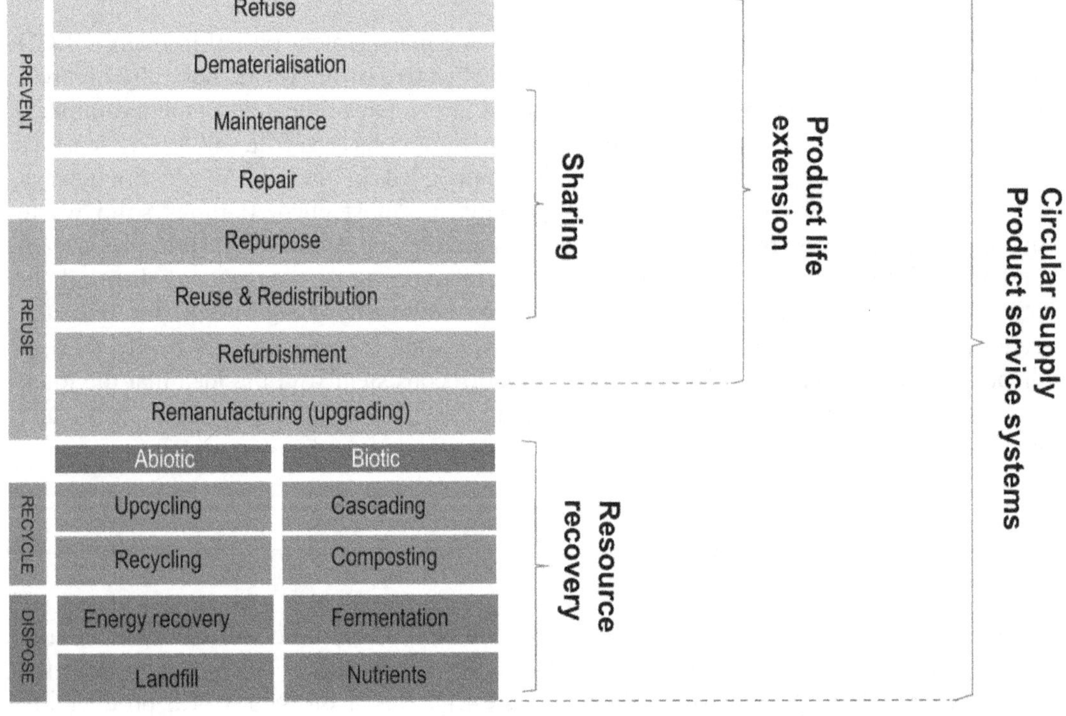

Source: Adapted from De Groene and Ethica (2015[2]), *Boosting circular design for a circular economy*, https://bit.ly/2phG1jl

4.3. Insights from the Life Cycle Assessment (LCA) literature

This section presents insights on the environmental footprints of different circular business models from the LCA studies (Box 4.2). This literature is extensive for some of the resource recovery, product life extension, and product service system business models, and the selection presented here should not be considered to be exhaustive. The circular supply and sharing business models have received relatively little attention in the LCA literature. In this section, the likely environmental footprint of circular supply models is therefore discussed alongside those for the resource recovery business model. The rationale for this is that these two business models, from an environmental perspective, can be seen as two sides to the same coin. The former involves product manufacturers switching to bio-based and/or recovered inputs while the latter involves the provision of some of these inputs. Finally, the discussion of the environmental footprint of sharing models, in the absence of LCA data, is more general and based on the underlying characteristics of that business model.

Box 4.2. Life cycle analysis: a brief summary

Life Cycle Assessment (LCA) is an internationally standardized methodology for establishing the environmental footprint of a particular product (good or service). Within the requirements of ISO 14040 and 14044, an LCA must comprise the following steps (WRAP, 2010[3]):

Goal and scope definition which defines the goal and intended use of the LCA, and scopes the assessment concerning system boundaries, function and flow, required data quality, technology and assessment parameters,

Inventory analysis (LCI) which consists in collecting data on inputs (resources and intermediate products) and outputs (emissions, wastes) for all the processes in the product system.

Impact assessment (LCIA), phase during which inventory data on inputs and outputs are translated into indicators of potential impacts on the environment, on human health, and on the availability of natural resources.

Interpretation of results where the results of the LCI and LCIA are interpreted according to the goal of the study and where sensitivity and uncertainty analysis are performed to qualify the results and the conclusions.

A LCA can either be undertaken for a product in isolation, or for one product relative to another. This distinction is important in the context of this chapter, which seeks to establish the environmental footprint of circular modes of production, either relative to other circular modes (recycling vs remanufacturing), or relative to more traditional modes (recycling vs primary material production). Because their underlying scope and assumptions often differ, it is generally difficult to compare the results from different LCA studies. As such, the data presented here are taken mostly from individual studies that effectively compare two LCAs: one for the footprint of the "circular" product, and one for the footprint of the "traditional" product. This is the origin of indicators like avoided resource extraction, energy use, and waste disposal.

Relative to the circularity ladder approach,[2] the key strengths of LCA are its transparent methodology and its capacity to provide quantitative results. It is possible to assess the potential magnitude of the change in environmental footprint as well as its general direction. With respect to the mainly "comparative" LCAs considered in this chapter, the main weakness relates to assumptions about the nature of the counterfactual. For example, it is often assumed, when calculating the environmental impact of recycling, that the resulting unit of secondary output displaces one unit of primary output further upstream.[3] This allows estimates of avoided material and energy extraction to be made, and these can then be converted into changes in global warming, acidification, eutrophication, and toxicity potential. As discussed further in Section 4.4, the extent to which output associated with circular modes of production actually displaces that associated with traditional production is largely determined by economic mechanisms.[4] Assuming a one to one displacement of traditional output may be overly optimistic, especially when rebound and other indirect economic effects are accounted for.

4.3.1. Circular supply and resource recovery business models

General environmental considerations

Relative to a scenario involving disposal, transforming waste into secondary materials and using them as new inputs is widely considered to have positive first order environmental effects. By diverting waste towards recovery facilities, resource recovery business models reduce the volume of material that requires landfilling or incineration, and therefore the environmental impacts of these activities. Similarly, by increasing the supply of secondary materials, resource recovery business models can reduce demand for primary resources, and the environmental impacts associated with their extraction. Further, producing finished materials from waste typically requires considerably less energy and, depending on the energy mix, greenhouse gas emissions than doing so from virgin resources. For example, secondary copper and aluminum production requires only around 35% and 5% of the energy used in the respective primary processes (BIR, 2008[4]).

LCA data: the example of recycling

There are a vast number of LCAs that assess the environmental footprint of recycling relative to other end of life solid waste management options. Various meta-analyses of this body of work have been undertaken and, in some cases, comprise as many as several hundred individual studies (Table 4.1). Some meta-analyses focus on a particular material; plastics (HPRC, 2015[5]; Bernardo, Simões and Pinto, 2016[6]), paper and cardboard (EEA, 2006[7]; NCASI, 2012[8]), and organic waste (Morris, Matthews and Morawski, 2012[9]) are all common. Others focus on either a variety of materials (WRAP, 2010[10]; Valerio, 2010[11]; DSEWPC, 2012[12]; Laurent et al., 2014[13]), or on a composite waste product like municipal solid waste (Cleary, 2009[14]). In terms of the environmental impact categories considered, most individual studies assess the effect of recycling on resource consumption, energy use, and greenhouse gas emissions. Some studies also assess the impacts on acidification and eutrophication potential, eco-toxicity, and avoided solid waste disposal. Less than 20% of LCAs on solid waste management assess impacts on land and water use (Laurent et al., 2014[13]).

Table 4.1. Selected literature assessing the environmental impacts of recycling

Study	Material focus	# studies	Environmental impact categories
EEA (2006[7])	Paper and Cardboard	9	Resource consumption, energy use, GWP, AP, toxicity, solid waste
WRAP (2006[15])	Various	55	Resource consumption, energy use, water use, GWP
Cleary (2009[14])	Waste	20	Energy use, GWP, AP
WRAP (2010[10])	Various	>200	Resource consumption, energy use, water use, GWP
Valerio (2010[11])	Various	31	GWP, AP, EP, PCOP, toxicity
NCASI (2012[8])	Paper	41	?
DSEWPC (2012[12])	Various	5	Resource consumption, energy use, water use, GWP, EP, PCOP, solid waste
Morris et al. (2012[9])	Organics	82	GWP, AP, human toxicity, eco toxicity
Astrup et al. (2015[16])	Waste	250	?
Laurent et al. (2014[13])	Various	222	Varies according to individual study
HPRC (2015[5])	Plastics	17	GWP, AP, EP
Bernardo et al. (2016[6])	Plastics	20	Energy use, GWP

Note: GWP = global warming potential, AP = acidification potential, EP = eutrophication potential, PCOP = Photochemical oxidation potential
Source: Various

The assumptions underlying individual LCAs vary considerably; a useful summary is provided by Laurent et al. (2014[13]). One key issue relates to the multi-functional character of material and energy recovery processes. For example, the environmental impacts of recycling result from both its waste management function (avoided disposal) as well as its role in the production of secondary commodities (avoided virgin resource extraction and processing). Assumptions about the volume (how much waste is recovered as opposed to disposed of?) and type (how substitutable are the recovered secondary materials for their primary equivalents?) of avoided resource extraction will significantly influence results. According to Laurent et al. (2014[13]), "most reviewed studies assume a substitution ratio of 1:1 and/or a quality similar to the substituted product". By ignoring the existence of down-cycling, this approach can lead to overestimates of the environmental benefits resulting from material recovery.[5] Other key issues that are highlighted include the treatment of capital goods (are the environmental impacts associated with the construction of material recovery infrastructure accounted for?), and collection and transport (are the environmental impacts associated with these activities accounted for?).

The key high level conclusion that emerges from the meta-analyses presented in Table 4.1 is that recycling has a small environmental footprint relative to traditional disposal activities.[6] WRAP (2006[15]) assessed 55 "state of the art" LCAs of paper and cardboard, glass, plastics, aluminium, steel, wood, and aggregates, and conclude that "most studies show that recycling offers more environmental benefits and lower environmental impacts than the other waste management options". On the basis of 222 individual studies, Laurent et al. (2014[13]) state that " … for waste paper, all studies favour recycling or thermal treatment over landfilling" and " … a relatively large proportion of studies tend to favour recycling over landfilling and thermal processes for plastics and paper". Bernardo, Simoes and Pinto (2016[6]) focussed on LCAs of plastics and found that "the results reported are generally consistent, showing that recycling has the lowest environmental impact on Global Warming Potential (GWP) and Total Energy Use (TEU) impacts".

Several of the meta-analyses present caveats to the conclusion that the environmental footprint of recycling is smaller than that for traditional disposal. Some caveats relate to specific materials. WRAP (2010[10]) state that, "for wood and textiles, more studies are needed to be able to make firmer conclusions regarding the environmental benefits of recycling". Other caveats relate to data limitations. NCASI (2012[8]) state that, "while many of the reviewed studies resulted in findings that suggest a lower LCA profile for recovery for recycling over landfilling as an end-of-life option for paper, the applicability of this finding is limited, given the extent to which it depends on assumptions regarding paper degradation in landfills and the methods used to account for biogenic carbon, and the relative weakness of current LCA toxicity-related impact assessment".

It is also apparent from the existing literature that the environmental impacts of recycling vary significantly across materials. Figure 4.2 shows data from a LCA undertaken in New South Wales, Australia by the Department of Environment, Climate Change, and Water (NSW EPA, 2010[17]). Recycling of metals is shown to have considerably larger environmental benefits in terms of avoided greenhouse gas emissions, energy use, and water use than recycling of building materials, paper and cardboard, organics, glass, or plastics. This is probably a function of the extremely high energy and water intensity of crushing, beneficiating, and refining mineral ores into finished metal products.

Figure 4.2. Average net environmental benefits of recycling 1 tonne of waste in Australia

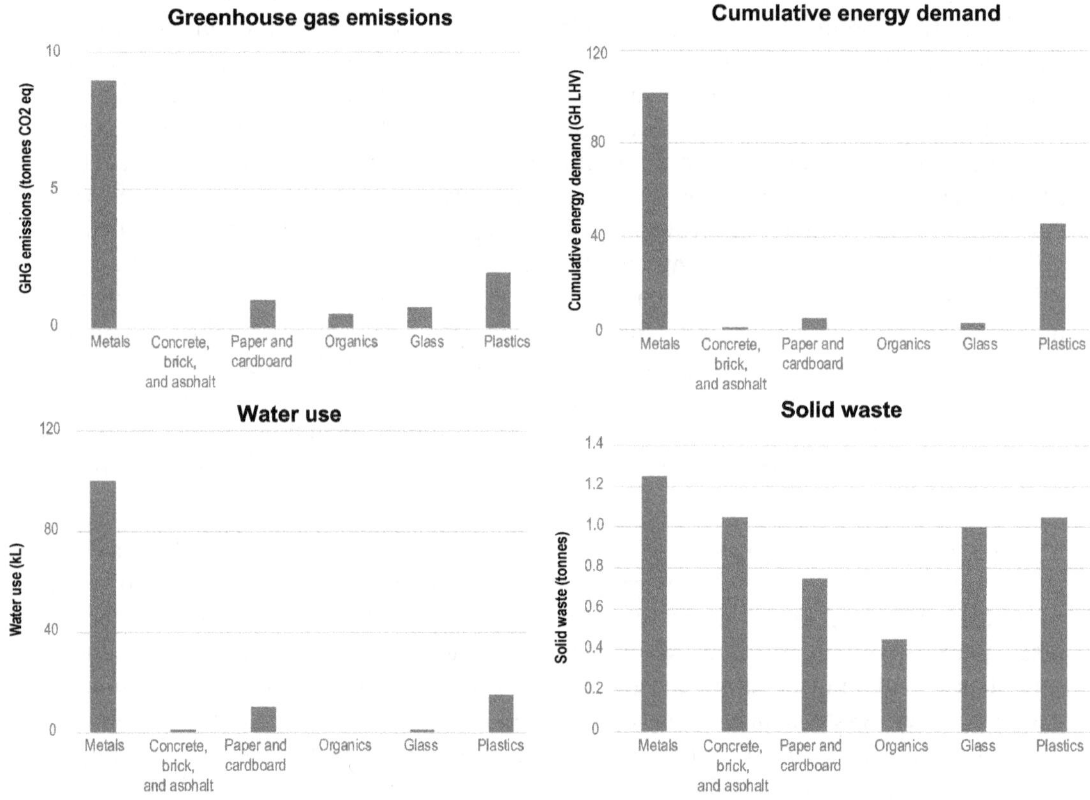

Source: NSW EPA (2010[17]), *Environmental benefits of recycling*, https://bit.ly/2xihXl2

Finally, the environmental impacts of recycling are also likely to vary significantly with recycling rates. This issue is raised by Ekvall (2007[18]), who state that "the environmental burdens of collection and recycling are likely to be a non-linear function of the collection rate", and, "at very high recycling rates, the required extra transport and processing of materials may increase fuel consumption and emissions greatly for each additional tonne of material that is collected". In more concrete terms, it is easy to imagine that the environmental benefits of collecting recyclable materials from smaller rural communities and transporting them to distant processing centres could require more energy use than it saves. This, in tandem with the private costs and benefits of recycling, raises the possibility of an optimum recycling rate. For example, cost benefit analysis undertaken for Japan finds that the recycling rate that minimises the average social cost[7] of municipal solid waste management is around 10%, which is significantly less than current recycling rates of 20% (Kinnaman, Shinkuma and Yamamoto, 2014[19]). Optimum recycling rates are likely to evolve over time as new technologies emerge and market prices change.

4.3.2. Product life extension models

General environmental considerations

Product life extension business models, whether classic long life, direct reuse, maintenance and repair, or refurbishment and remanufacturing, tend to slow the flow of products and materials through the economy. This is widely considered to be positive from an environmental viewpoint. Reduced demand for new products translates up the value chain into reduced extraction and processing of new resources, and down the value chain into reduced disposal. The associated environmental impact of these activities is thereby reduced.

There are at least three second order factors that may, at least partially, offset such environmental gains.[8] First, the average environmental footprint of in-use products may increase if longer lived products slow the diffusion of new, relatively efficient designs. This is of particular concern for product categories characterized by large use phase impacts and rapid technological progress.[9] Second, with the exception of the classic long life business model, product life extension processes also require inputs of materials and energy. For example, the environmental footprint of transporting a product to a repair or remanufacturing facility may be non-negligible. Third, if choosing repaired, second-hand, or remanufactured goods creates significant consumer savings, then there will also be potential for rebound effects. Essentially, the additional consumption resulting from increased disposable income also has an environmental footprint.

These three concerns apply to different extents for each of the four product life extension sub-models. For example, because higher prices are central to the classic long life business model, there is little potential for direct rebound effects. Further, because this business model (when considered in isolation) dispels with the need for post-sales repair or remanufacture, it also negates the environmental footprint of these activities (transport for example). As such, the classic long life business model has considerable potential from an environmental perspective, especially for product categories (such as clothing) where a low proportion of the lifecycle environmental footprint is associated with the use-phase (see DEFRA (2011[20]) for further discussion). More generally, it is unclear from the existing literature to what extent the environmental benefits associated with longer lived products (reduced extraction and processing of new resources, reduced disposal of end of life products) are offset by second order effects.

LCA data: the example of remanufacturing

There are a considerable number of LCAs that assess the environmental footprint of product remanufacturing, typically relative to a scenario involving product disposal and the purchase of an equivalent new product. The product focus in these studies is diverse, but common categories include automobiles (and their constituent parts), imaging equipment, and printer cartridges. A selection of this literature is presented in Table 4.2. Most studies focus on a limited subset of impact categories. Avoided energy use and greenhouse gas emissions are the most common, and avoided resource extraction and waste disposal are also occasionally assessed.

Table 4.2. Selected literature assessing the environmental impacts of remanufacturing

Author	Study type	Product Focus	Change in resource extraction	Change in energy consumption	Change in GHG emissions	Waste disposal
Kerr and Ryan (2001[21])	LCA	Photocopiers	-19% to -25%	-27%	-23%	-35%
		Photocopiers (modular)	-39% to -48%	-68%	-65%	-47%
Smith and Keoleian (2004[22])	LCA	Engines	-26% to -90%	-68% to -83%	-73% to -87%	-65% to -88%
Steinhilper (1998[23])	?	Various	-	-85%	-	-
Neto and Bloemhof (2009[24])	LCA	Personal computers	-	-80%	-	-
Kara (2010[25])	LCA	Printer cartridges	-	-	-33%	-
Gutowski et al. (2011[26])	Meta-review	Furniture	-	-100%	-	-
		Clothing	-	-64%	-	-
		Computers	-	-57%	-	-
		Electric motors	-	3%	-	-
		Tires	-	9%	-	-
		Appliances	-	75%	-	-
		Engines	-	-4%	-	-
		Toner cartridges	-	-6%	-	-
Warsen et al. (2011[27])	LCA	Gearbox	>50%	-33%	-	-
Biswas and Rosano (2011[28])	LCA	Compressors	-	-	-90%	-
Liu et al. (2014[29])	LCA	Engines	-95%	-66%	-67%	-
Wilson et al. (2014[30])	LCA	Turbine blades	-	-36%	-45%	-
ERN (2015[31])	Meta-review	Aerospace	-	-	-356,000	-136,000
		Automotive	-	-	-3,298,000	-902,000
		EEE	-	-	-177,000	-150,000
		Furniture	-	-	-131,000	-76,000
		Heavy duty equipment	-	-	-3,458,000	-855,000
		Machinery	-	-	-393,000	-35,000
		Marine	-	-	-40,000	-15,000
		Medical equipment	-	-	-58,000	-22,000
		Rail	-	-	-344,000	-69,000
Gao et al. (2017[32])	LCA	Turbochargers	-	-82.50%	-73%	-

Note: Change in GHG emissions and waste disposal in ERN (2015[31]) are at the European level due to current remanufacturing rates.

Note: The International Resource Panel is undertaking a major research project on remanufacturing, refurbishment, repair, and direct reuse. Among other outputs, this work includes calculations of the environmental impacts of life extension activities in the automobile, heavy machinery, and imaging equipment sectors. Final results were unavailable at the time of writing.

Source: Various

The key conclusion that emerges from the LCA literature is that remanufacturing can result in sectoral reductions in resource extraction and waste disposal that are often in the order of 80%. This, in turn, will translate into a variety of environmental impacts. The one that is most frequently evaluated in the literature is the avoided greenhouse gas emissions associated with extraction and processing of virgin resources into new products. Although the sectoral reductions in resource extraction, energy consumption, and greenhouse gas emissions shown in Table 4.2 seem large, they are consistent with the nature of remanufacturing. In many cases, it is the deterioration of a small number of parts or components, rather than a failure of the product itself, that leads to a loss of functionality. Remanufacturing worn out parts, while retaining the core of the original product, can therefore prevent the loss of a high proportion of the constituent materials, along with their embedded energy content.

As discussed in the introduction to this section, there are at least three second order effects that may partially offset the upstream environmental benefits associated with longer lived products. Two of these – the environmental footprint of transporting used cores, and the potential for rebound effects resulting from consumer savings – are largely ignored in the remanufacturing LCAs considered here. Further, most of the LCAs in Table 4.2 appear to assume zero recycling rates in their "disposal and buy a new product scenario" when, in reality, significant proportions of some end of life products are recycled (the chassis' of end of life vehicles for example).

Gutowski et al. (2011[26]) is the only study considered here that accounts for the impact of remanufacturing on the diffusion of new product designs.[10] One important conclusion that emerges from this work is that, for certain product categories, the relatively poor energy efficiency of retained (remanufactured) products can more than offset the energy savings associated with reduced material production and traditional manufacturing (e.g. Figure 4.3: products 20 to 25 – dishwashers, monitor screens, refrigerators, and some computers). The authors highlight that this risk is greatest for long-lived product categories characterised by high use-phase energy requirements and rapid efficiency improvements.

Figure 4.3. Life cycle energy use of remanufactured products relative to new equivalents

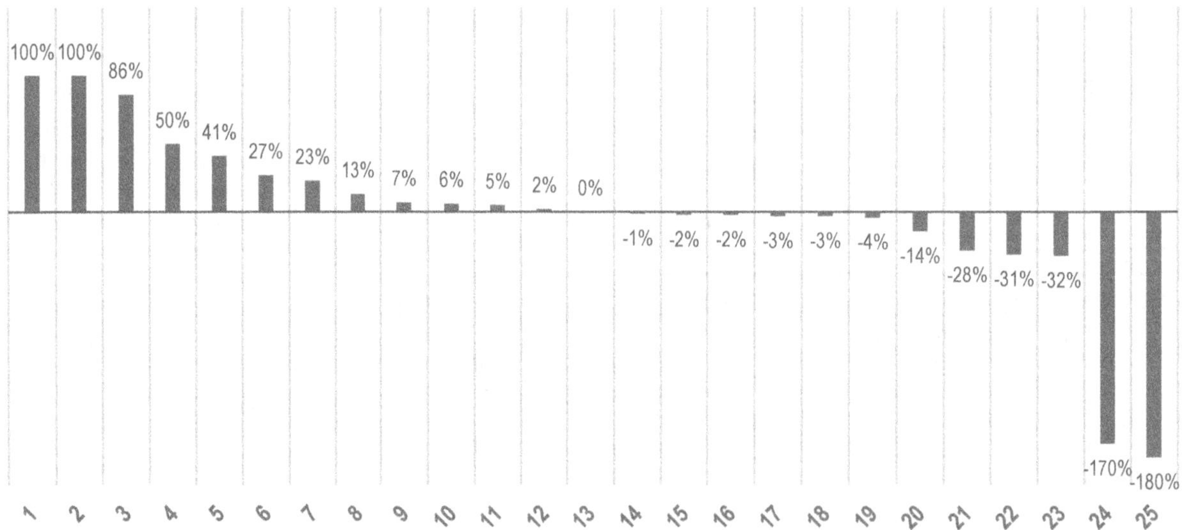

Note: Furniture (1 and 2), textiles (3 and 5), appliances (20, 23, 25), computers (4, 6, 7, 8, 21, 24), toner cartridge (10), engines (11, 12), electric engines (13, 14, 15, 17, 18, 19), tires (9, 22, 16).

In sum, remanufacturing, like other product life extension business models, leads to avoided resource extraction, processing, and disposal; the environmental damages resulting from these associated with these activities will therefore be reduced. What is less clear from this review is the extent to which these environmental benefits are offset by various second order effects, especially those associated with the use phase of the product life cycle.[11] Because remanufacturing keeps existing products in circulation for longer, it may also slow the diffusion of new and relatively efficient product designs. Caution in promoting manufacturing is warranted when the affected product categories are characterized by: (i) long product lives, (ii) energy or water intensive during the use phase, and (iii) high rates of efficiency improvements.

4.3.3. Sharing models

General environmental considerations

Sharing models are based upon short term rental transactions of under-utilised economic assets or goods. They provide consumers with additional choice: instead of buying goods from a traditional business provider, it is possible to temporarily lease them from an individual. In terms of the environmental implications of this shift, there is a widely held view that, by facilitating the use of under-utilised goods, sharing models will have positive environmental impacts. Many platforms advertise themselves as green, and particularly as carbon-footprint reducing (e.g., Frenken and Schor, 2017 ([33])). Consumers often appear to share this opinion. A survey undertaken by PWC in 2016 found that 76% of surveyed individuals believed that "the sharing economy is better for the environment" (PWC, 2015[34]). Further, a survey undertaken by Bocker and Meelen (2017[35]) found that this perceived greenness was a key motivation for participating in certain sectors of the sharing economy.[12]

The idea underlying these attitudes seems to be that lower demand for new goods can reduce virgin resource extraction, material processing, and manufacturing, and therefore the environmental impacts associated with these activities. While there is likely to be some substance to this idea, the academic literature on these effects is more equivocal. There is little empirical evidence that sharing business models are, by definition, positive from an environmental viewpoint. Box 4.3 provides key conclusions from a set of recent assessments.

Box 4.3. Environmental impacts of sharing models: evidence from recent assessments

IDDRI (2014[36]): "the environmental impact of these (sharing) practices, in the way that they have developed today, is rarely obvious and there are many reasons to raise doubts: a degree of pragmatism is required" … and … "In particular, the analysis of the sustainability of the (sharing) models is hampered by the lack of studies and its dissemination. To quote the candid remarks of one expert, "it is hard to reason on the basis of very poor statistical data."

The Economist (2015): "In many cases, the benefits of sharing economy services are that they reduce cost and improve convenience—both of which might, in fact, boost consumption".

European Commission (2016[37]): "Available empirical evidence to date is very partial and inconclusive - in many cases, it is simply anecdotal and often presented by stakeholders in the current controversies. For example, Uber and Airbnb have released dozens of reports, the reliability of which could not be independently validated because the methodologies are not transparently illustrated and data are kept internal and not made accessible to researchers".

Sierra Club (2017[38]): "Many well-meaning, environment-friendly people have bought the line that the sharing economy is green" and "When it comes to the "greenness" of the sharing economy, magical thinking and corporate press releases have replaced fact-based discourse".

ADEME (2016[39]): "Collaborative consumption does not necessarily signify responsible consumption. Indeed, the environmental gain depends strongly on the traditional activity that the collaborative activity replaces."

Trinomics (2017[40]): "To date, little objective and thorough research has been done on the true environmental impacts of the collaborative economy. Many studies only use anecdotal evidence or only took into account direct and indirect environmental impacts, but not the rebound effect, that is the effect of increased consumption because of a decrease in prices, extra money earned and saved through engaging in the collaborative economy instead of the traditional economy".

Nordic Council of Ministers (2017[41]): "More efficient use of the resources through sharing initiatives could also contribute to environmental benefits, but this depends on how people change their behaviour and spend their savings from using the initiatives."

Although robust data are unavailable, the environmental impacts associated with the continued emergence of sharing models will depend largely on at least three factors: (i) the effect that increased utilisation rates have on goods' expected lifetimes, (ii) the composition of the additional consumption resulting from any financial savings,[13] and (iii) the existence of any differences in the life-cycle environmental footprint of shared and traditional goods (e.g., IDDRI, 2014 ([36])). Given the previously mentioned lack of empirical data, the remainder of this section focusses on discussing each of these factors.

The effect that increased utilisation of spare capacity will have on demand for new goods, and therefore on demand for virgin resource inputs, will depend on how increased utilisation affects the expected lifetime of the relevant goods. If the expected life of a good is strongly related to how frequently it is used, then any increase in utilisation rates will lead to shorter product lives, more rapid product turnover, and a limited impact on overall demand.[14] This scenario is probably most relevant for products like vehicles or personal computers. In contrast, if the expected life of a good is not strongly related to how frequently it is used (consider housing or household tools for example), then increased utilisation may well lead to reduced demand for new production.

Consumer surveys suggest that a key motivation for participating in the peer to peer markets is the availability of considerable savings (Böcker and Meelen, 2017[35]). In concrete terms, it is considerably cheaper for consumers to satisfy demand for goods, mobility, and short stay accommodation through leasing rather than buying. The resulting financial savings can result in a rebound effect, where the environmental footprint of new consumption at least partially offsets any environmental benefits resulting from sharing. Relatedly, there is some (mostly anecdotal) evidence that the earning opportunities made possible by the emergence of sharing models are actually stimulating investment in new capacity in certain markets. For example, it seems likely that some of the vehicles used by Uberpool drivers, and some of the apartments leased by Airbnb hosts, would never have been purchased in the absence of those platforms. Keeping these considerations in mind is important when considering the overall environmental impact of sharing models (especially the avoided resource extraction and processing associated with the displacement of traditional providers).

If shared goods and their traditionally marketed equivalents were identical, then the two factors discussed above would probably determine much of the environmental impact of sharing models. However, in reality, the goods involved are often not identical, and this means that they can have differing environmental footprints. This effect can work in both directions. For example, in the context of mobility, the shared vehicles that are listed on peer to peer platforms like Getaround are likely to have a higher emissions signature than the vehicles leased by traditional car rental agencies. In contrast, in the context of short term lodging, it is often argued that the rooms listed on platforms like Airbnb have a smaller energy and water footprint than those in traditional hotels (see below).

LCA and survey data: the example of sharing under-utilised accommodation

As noted above, there is little systematic research that has assessed the environmental impacts of sharing models. What does exist often focusses on these business models in the short term lodging segment of the hospitality sector. This section presents three such assessments. Some of this work has been commissioned by the platform operators themselves; the results should be interpreted with that in mind.

A 2016 study undertaken by the World Economic Forum (WEF) and the Massachusetts Institute of Technology (MIT) assesses the material savings that might be associated with the emergence of accommodation sharing (WEF, 2016[42]). Researchers were interested in the role that Airbnb played in Rio de Janeiro before, during, and after the 2014 Football World Cup and 2016 Olympic Games. The authors found that short-term Airbnb leases housed around 17% of the estimated 500 000 tourists who visited Rio de Janeiro during the Olympic Games. This was calculated to represent the equivalent of 257 newly built hotels, each of which "would have been a large undertaking in terms of financing and material use". This study was a preliminary effort, but does serve to highlight two of the shortcomings that are common to other assessments of sharing models. First, by overlooking economic mechanisms, it probably overestimates the impact that Airbnb had on hotel construction and, by extension, on resource extraction and use.[15] Second, this estimate of avoided resource extraction and use is not extended to more tangible environmental impact categories such as global warming, acidification, and toxicity potential. Not all resource extraction is necessarily "bad"; the impacts involved will vary significantly according to the types of materials involved and where they are extracted and processed.

A 2014 study commissioned by AirBnb focusses more on the comparative use phase environmental impacts of shared and traditional (hotel) short term accommodation (Cleantech, 2014[43]). The research was based on 8 000 survey respondents in Europe and North America; jurisdictions which currently make up the vast majority of Airbnb stays. The study found that Airbnb guests in these two geographic areas use 63 - 84% less energy and 12 – 57% less water per guest night than typical hotel guests.[16] Based on 92% of the respondents reporting that they produced an equal or lower amount of waste than when at home, it was also concluded that Airbnb stays produce 28-53% less waste than hotel stays. On the basis of these reductions, it was calculated that Airbnb stays in Europe resulted in annual greenhouse gas savings equivalent to removing 200 000 cars from the road and annual water use savings equivalent to 1 100 Olympic size swimming pools.

A 2017 study undertaken by the Agence de l'Environnement et de la Matrise de l'Energie (ADEME) also assesses short term sharing relative to traditional hotel rooms (ADEME, 2016[39]). The authors find that the differential environmental impacts of this choice are difficult to evaluate because of the number of factors that require consideration. The importance of individual behaviour, the relative sizes of rooms and apartments associated with Airbnb and hotel stays, and the electricity mix in different host countries are all factors that need to be considered. One firm conclusion provided by ADEME is that the sharing of under-utlilised capacity in the short term lodging segment is most likely to be environmentally beneficial when it involves individual rooms rather than entire apartments. In this situation, the energy and water use required for lighting, heating, and cleaning will be shared across more than one individual.

4.3.4. Product-service systems

General considerations

Product service systems change patterns of asset ownership. Instead of purchasing a good or asset, consumers purchase the service(s) that the good or service provides: actual ownership often remains with the original manufacturer. This characteristic of PSS creates a new set of incentives around product design, product use, and product disposal, with associated implications for the life-cycle environmental footprint of affected goods.

From a manufacturer's perspective, the adoption of the user-oriented or result-oriented PSS variants means assuming responsibility for product disposal at the end of life. In a similar way to extended producer responsibility schemes, this can create an incentive to design products that are amenable to life extension processes such as remanufacture, refurbishment, or repair. This incentive, which is likely to be positive from an environmental viewpoint, may be at least partially offset by three opposing effects.

It has been suggested that concerns about cannibalizing rentals of relatively new product lines can lead PSS providers to prematurely remove old products from the market. Agrawal et al. (2012[44]) argue that such behavior could contribute to shorter product lives relative to a situation where individuals seek to sell, rather than dispose of assets (e.g. cars in the second hand car market).

It is possible that consumers use leased goods less carefully than goods that they own (Kuo, 2011[45]) which, if true, would also contribute to shorter product lives.

As discussed in Section 3.3, the environmental implications of longer lived products are not entirely clear; the upstream environmental benefits resulting from any reduction in demand for virgin resources may be partially offset by an increased environmental footprint in the use phase.

The adoption of PSS also creates other environmentally favourable incentives. For manufacturers producing consumable goods like energy and chemicals, the adoption of the result-oriented PSS variant will create incentives for their more efficient use. This is nicely explained by (Tukker, 2015[46]), who states that "in result-oriented business models, the use of materials also becomes merely a cost factor – using more materials or creating more products does not lead to increased revenues". In addition, from a consumer perspective, the pay for use tariff structure of the user-oriented PSS variant may create incentives for more efficient product use. Because the variable cost of product use is more prominent than when products are owned, there will be a tendency to use them relatively sparingly.

User-oriented PSS business models are also being increasingly adopted in the context of digital products: e-books, streamed music and film, and digital media. This has potentially significant environmental impacts because the material basis for these products becomes unnecessary. A subscription to Spotify or an online media outlet provides access to music and news without the need for CDs or newspapers. The key question in this context is the extent to which the associated reductions in resource extraction, processing, and eventual product disposal are offset by the increased resource mobilisation required for the development of digital infrastructure (data servers and cable networks) and personal electronic devices. Establishing the net environmental impact is challenging because of the different materials involved.

Despite the existence of a considerable body of work on the environmental implications of PSS, there is little empirical evidence that they result in tangibly lower environmental pressure. The most comprehensive meta-analysis to date (Tukker, 2015[46]) concludes that "PSS will not by definition be more resource-efficient or 'circular' than product systems" but that "result-oriented PSS offers the greatest prospect of radical resource efficiency gains". Currently operating examples of result-oriented – chemical leasing (e.g., OECD, 2017 ([47])) or lighting or heating service contracts – are therefore worthy of additional attention. It is also likely that the environmental implications of the emergence of PSS will depend on the product category affected. Agrawal et al. (2012[44]) and Intlekofer, Bras and Ferguson (2010[48]) find that environmental benefits are more likely to emerge when the product category involved is characterized by high use phase impacts and rapid technological progress. The following example therefore focusses on PSS as applied to urban car sharing.

LCA and survey data: the example of urban car sharing schemes

There is a considerable body of work that assesses the environmental impacts of car sharing. A selection of this literature is presented in Table 4.3. Most studies focus on the environmental impacts related to vehicle ownership and use. Vehicle kilometers travelled (VKT) and the associated greenhouse gas emissions, along with the number of privately owned cars replaced by each shared vehicle are the most common impact categories. Changes in vehicle kilometers travelled are often viewed as a proxy for energy extraction and use, or for particulate emissions in urban environments. The number of privately owned cars replaced is viewed as having implications for urban land use patterns, congestion, and virgin resource extraction rates (see below). Few studies consider the potential rebound effect associated with savings resulting from car sharing. This new consumption will tend to offset any gains associated with shared mobility.

Most studies assessing the environmental impacts of car sharing use consumer surveys to establish how the existence of a car sharing scheme changes vehicle ownership and mobility decisions. Car sharing members are asked a variety of questions about how their driving behavior, vehicle ownership, and use of other transport modes change due to the introduction of a car sharing scheme. Typically, respondents are presented with a before and after scenario; they are asked to compare their current behavior with a counterfactual based on recollections of their past behavior.[17] It is important to keep in mind the shortcomings of such an approach. First, individuals' recollections of their past behavior may deviate from their actual behavior; any systematic deviation will tend to bias the results of the subsequent analysis. Second, the current behavior of surveyed individuals is unlikely to be entirely attributable to the introduction of a vehicle sharing scheme. For example, changes in fuel prices are also likely to affect transport decisions.[18]

The vehicles available through car sharing schemes are not necessarily representative of the wider vehicle fleet. They are often smaller and are increasingly electric, and may therefore have lower environmental impacts relative to an "average" private vehicle. Some studies incorporate this effect via life cycle analysis. This approach is typically of limited scope, focusing mostly on the differential energy use and greenhouse gas emissions associated with the use phase of the vehicle life. Any differential environmental impacts associated with vehicle manufacturing and disposal are largely ignored (although see Doka and Ziegler, 2001 ([49])).

Table 4.3. Selected literature assessing the environmental impacts of car sharing

Author	Methodology	Average change in VKT	Average change in mobility related GHG emissions	Private cars replaced
Doka and Ziegler (2001[49])	LCA	-	-39%	-
Lane (2005[50])	Survey	-	-	23
Millard-Ball et al. (2005[51])	?	-37%	-	15
Ryder and Morin (2005[52])	Survey	-28% to -48%	-39% to -54%	-
Cervero et al. (2007[53])	Survey	-33%	-	-
MOMO (2010[54])	Meta-review	-	-8% to -36%	4 to 14
Martin et al. (2011[55]) Martin and Shaheen (2011[56])	Survey	-	-15%	9 to 13
Firnkorn and Muller (2011[57])	Survey	-	-	11
Stasko et al. (2013[58])	Survey	-	-	15
Martin and Shaheen (2016[59])	Survey	-6% to -16%	-4% to -18%	7 to 11
Chen and Kockelman (2016[60])	Meta-review	-27% to -67%	-51%	-
Nijland and van Meerkerk (2017[61])	Survey	-15% to -20%	-13% to -18%	-

Note: Changes in average VKT and mobility related GHG emissions are for survey respondents only (i.e. members of car sharing schemes). Changes in average mobility related GHG emissions reflect differing combinations of: (i) the lower emissions intensity of car sharing vehicles, (ii) changed driving behavior resulting from access to a car sharing scheme, and (iii) associated shifts in transport modes.
Source: Various

Results from individual studies shown in Table 4.3 are not directly comparable. The boundary of each analysis varies, as do assumptions about key parameters. For example, in estimating the impact of car sharing on transport related GHG emissions, some studies restrict their analysis to the impact resulting purely from different car designs (e.g. Doka and Ziegler, 2001 ([49])), or purely from behavioral changes (e.g. Martin and Shaheen, 2011 ([56])). Further, the treatment of changes in transport modes resulting from the introduction of car sharing differs across studies. Some assessments account for emissions associated with shifts to other transport modes (e.g. Firnkorn and Muller, 2011 ([57])) whereas others ignore this effect on the basis that is likely to be small (e.g. Martin and Shaheen, 2011 ([56])). Finally, different types of car sharing are considered by different studies. Some assessments only consider one-way systems (e.g. Firnkorn and Muller, 2011 ([57])), others only consider roundtrip systems (e.g Millard-Ball et al. 2005 ([51])), and some (e.g. Nijland and van Meerkerk, 2017 ([61])) include both.

The environmental impact associated with the introduction of a car sharing scheme is consistent across the studies shown in Table 4.3. On average, members drive fewer kilometers, emit fewer GHG, and own fewer cars than they did previously. This aggregate outcome masks important variations in individual level behaviour. For example, various studies indicate that the majority of active car sharing members do not own a private vehicle. Around 58% of respondents in Martin, Shaheen and Lidicker

(2011[55]) said that they joined car sharing because they didn't have a car of their own. For this portion of the population, gaining access to a car sharing scheme probably serves to increase VKT (and probably also GHG emissions) as individuals shift away from other transport modes. The fact that overall VKT and GHG emissions fall appears to be, in large part, due to the behavior of a minority of car owning individuals. Survey data indicates that this portion of the population responds to the introduction of a car sharing scheme by reducing vehicle ownership and substituting shared mobility or other transport modes for private car ownership. Research by Martin and Shaheen (2011[56]) finds that the emissions reductions associated with this portion of the population more than offset the emissions increases associated with individuals without previous vehicle access (Figure 4.4).

Figure 4.4. Changes in mobility related to GHG emissions due to the introduction of a car sharing scheme

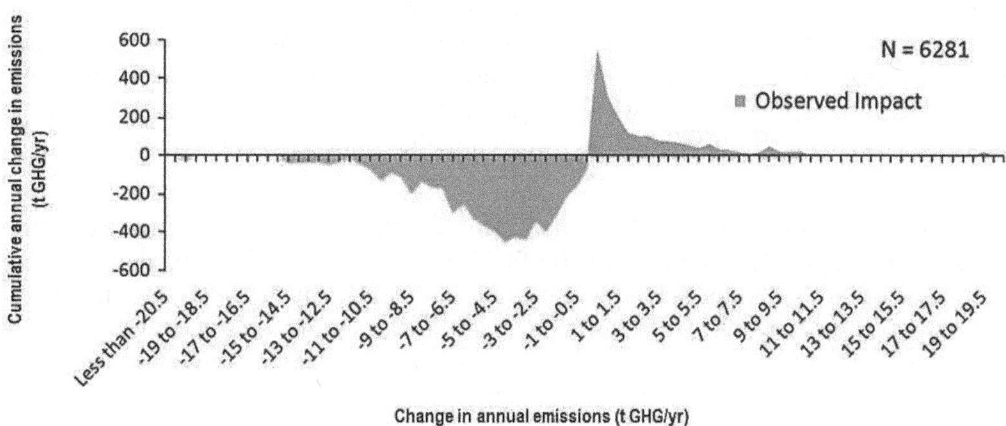

Note: Cumulative annual change in emissions represents the annual change in emissions made by each car sharing member multiplied by the number of individuals that make the same response.
Source: Martin and Shaheen (2011[56]).

The studies shown in Table 4.3 also indicate that having access to a car sharing scheme can lead to reduced rates of car ownership. This has at least two potential impacts on the environmental pressures associated with mobility. First, a smaller vehicle stock reduces demand for parking space. This can have positive environmental implications in urban areas where the sealing of bare ground can lower aquifer recharge rates and reduce resilience to storm events. Second, reduced vehicle demand may lead to lower rates or virgin resource extraction further upstream. This idea is controversial, it relies heavily on the assumption that demand reductions resulting from reduced private car ownership are not offset by any reduction in average vehicle life (i.e., due to high utilisation rates of shared vehicles). The net effect of car sharing on overall vehicle demand and resource extraction is uncertain without data on the average life of shared vehicles.

4.4. How economic feedbacks influence environmental outcomes

The LCA literature provides a valuable insight into the environmental footprint of circular products and modes of production relative to traditional equivalents. However, the actual environmental impact of circular business models will also depend on the output growth they can achieve, the extent to which this output displaces that associated with traditional production modes, and on the indirect effects that this has on the composition of the broader economy (Zink and Geyer, 2017[62]). Furthermore, the emergence of global value chains means that these broader effects are unlikely to be restricted to a particular jurisdiction, but will influence economic and environmental outcomes across borders. In sum, focussing solely on LCA studies alone may result in an incomplete view of the environmental potential of circular business models.

There is a growing literature of accounting studies that deal with this issue by combining results from LCA studies with assumptions about the market share that a circular business model could capture in the future. For example, TNO (2013[63]) find that increased recycling in the Dutch consumer electronics and food sectors could lead to emissions reductions of 747 000 tonnes and 150 000 tonnes of CO_2 per year respectively. Similarly, the Ellen Macarthur Foundation (2013[64]) find that higher reuse and remanufacturing rates for mobile phones in the EU could eradicate 1 300 000 tonnes of CO_2e annually. While these accounting approaches do give some indication of the overall environmental potential of a circular economy transition, they tend to ignore the economic realities that such a transition is conditional upon. In particular, it is often assumed that circular business models will scale up regardless of their underlying profitability, and that the new output will displace that associated with traditional production modes on a one-to-one basis. These assumptions, along with the fact that indirect economic effects are largely ignored, mean that the likelihood of achieving the stated environmental benefits is probably small.

Addressing the various market failures, policy misalignments, status quo biases, and other barriers (see Chapter 3) that hinder the profitability of circular business models will tend to stimulate future scale up. The environmental implications of this scale up will emerge through two main channels. Direct environmental impacts will result from the expansion of the new business model in a particular sector. Indirect environmental impacts will result from changes in the activity levels of other sectors of the economy in response to general equilibrium price effects. Establishing the overall environmental impact associated with the emergence of a circular business model requires consideration of both (Figure 4.5).

Figure 4.5. Direct and indirect impacts of addressing the barriers to circular business model adoption

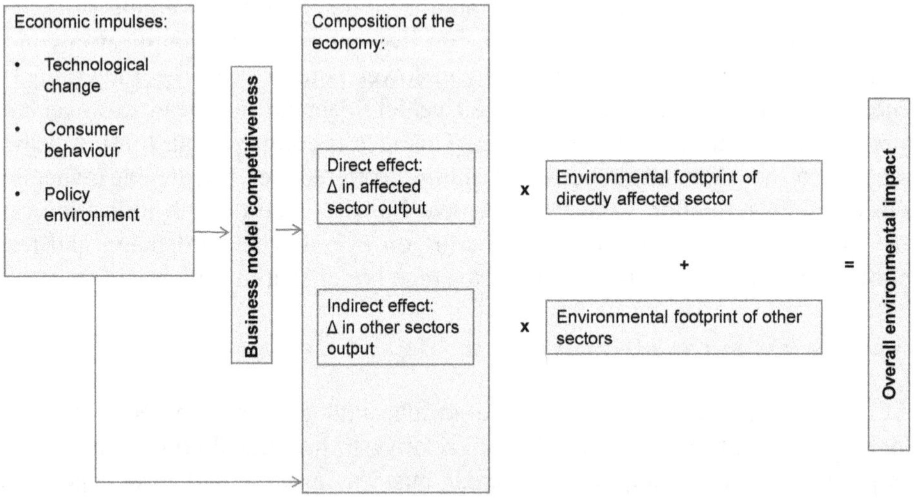

4.4.1. Direct environmental impacts of circular business model scale up

The selected LCA literature presented in this chapter indicates that the environmental footprint of circular products and circular modes of production is typically significantly smaller than for their traditional equivalents. By closing and slowing resource loops, and by narrowing resource flows, these business models reduce the extraction, transport, processing, and disposal of new resources, and the environmental pressures associated with these activities. For example, the existing LCAs focusing on remanufacturing find that it can save 80 to 90% of the energy that is required to manufacture certain types of new products. The direct environmental effect associated with the emergence of a circular business model will depend both on this difference in footprints, as well as on the extent to which traditional production is displaced.

As discussed, most LCA and accounting assessments of the environmental impact of circular business models assume that output from an emerging circular business model will displace that from a traditional business model on a one-to-one basis. This may be an overly optimistic assumption from an economic viewpoint, especially if the respective products are not perfect substitutes. For example, in the context of metal recycling, it is well established that secondary metals are less substitutable for their primary equivalents in certain high performance applications (Koffler et al., 2013[65]). Similarly, for sharing models, it is unlikely that short term lodging á la Airbnb is a perfect substitute for hotel rooms; many business travelers continue to prefer the convenience of the latter. Limited substitutability may mean that some circular products will be produced in addition, rather than instead of, traditional products (Zink and Geyer, 2017[62]).[19] If true, this implies that the overall direct environmental benefit of the growth of circular business models may be smaller than predicted.[20]

4.4.2. Indirect environmental impacts of circular business model scale up

The emergence of a circular business model in a particular sector cannot be considered in isolation. Increased activity will typically trigger changes in relative prices, thereby leading to spill-over and feedback effects elsewhere in the economy (Hertwich, 2005[66]). In terms of their environmental impact, these general equilibrium effects can act to "take back" the first order environmental gains associated with a particular business model.

Sorrell and Dimitripoulos (2008[67]) distinguish three types of indirect or general equilibrium economic effects:

Direct rebound effects occur when lower product prices, perhaps resulting from the emergence of a more resource efficient technology, mode of production, or product, lead to additional consumption. This often involves consumers. For example, although the fuel efficiency of vehicle engines has improved markedly over recent decades, the average fuel consumption per kilometre travelled has barely changed; consumers have opted to use the savings to buy larger and heavier vehicles. Direct rebound effects also involve firms. For example, increased penetration of heavy machinery remanufacturing will tend to reduce upstream resource extraction, but the resulting fall in prices may trigger additional demand for these materials from other production sectors.

Indirect effects occur when consumers allocate monetary savings, perhaps resulting from the emergence of a more resource efficient technology, mode of production, or product, to additional consumption of other goods and services (with an associated material and environmental footprint). For example, consumers may decide to allocate additional disposable income from sharing power tools (rather than buying them) to additional overseas travel.

Economy wide effects occur when the emergence of a more resource efficient technology, mode of production, or product triggers changes in the composition or size of the overall economy. For example, a number of modelling assessments indicate that resource efficiency and circular economy policies could generate significant economic growth (McCarthy, Dellink and Bibas, 2018[68]). This additional output will clearly have an associated material and environmental footprint.

The key message here is that gaining a better understanding of the overall environmental impact of circular economy business models requires considering the full range of dynamic and indirect economic feedbacks. Research in other fields has highlighted the potential importance of these mechanisms. Empirical assessments of the direct rebound effect in the context of energy efficiency improvements find that they are typically in the order of 15 to 30%, and occasionally as high as 50 to 60% (Hertwich, 2005[66]). Modelling assessments have also been undertaken, and often suggest that the size of the total rebound effect can exceed 50% (Dimitropoulos, 2007[69]; Koesler, Swales and Turner, 2016[70]; Parrado, Eni and Mattei, 2017[71]). The magnitude of these effects is quite striking given that they have been largely overlooked in assessments of the environmental impacts of circular business models. As stated in a recent review, "proponents of the circular economy have tended to look at the world purely as an engineering system and have overlooked the economic part of the circular economy" (Zink and Geyer, 2017[62]).

4.5. Conclusions

This chapter has highlighted the complexity involved in assessing the environmental impact of circular business models. Not only are there a wide range of business models involved, but there are also a variety of different approaches available to estimate their impacts. In addition, the impacts associated with each business model often emerge at different parts of the product lifecycle.[21] Based on the material presented in this chapter, it is possible to draw four main conclusions.

First, results from the LCA literature indicate that the environmental footprint of the output from circular modes of production can be significantly smaller than that associated with traditional modes. As such, the emergence of circular business models, to the extent that this results in the displacement of traditional forms of production, is likely to have a positive direct impact on environmental outcomes. By closing and slowing resource loops, and by narrowing resource flows, these business models will lead to less extraction, transport, processing, and disposal of virgin resources, and thereby reduce the environmental pressures associated with these activities.[22]

Second, the LCA and accounting studies presented here do not account for indirect economic effects associated with the emergence of circular business models. This emergence, conditional on improved competitiveness of circular modes of production, will place downward pressure on prices and are likely to lead to a range of rebound effects. Households may direct new disposable income towards additional consumption, and this will have an associated environmental footprint. Further, reduced demand for primary materials, and the lower prices that this stimulates, may encourage manufacturing firms to use relatively more such inputs. In sum, indirect economic feedbacks are important, and potentially could at least partially, offset the direct environmental benefits associated with the emergence of a circular business models.[23]

Third, comparing the relative environmental potential of different circular business models is difficult. Making such an assessment is difficult given that a particular business model typically operates in multiple sectors, and has implications across a range of environmental impact categories, often in multiple political jurisdictions. Thus, while it might be possible to compare the environmental footprint of recycling or repairing an old vehicle, blanket statements about the relative desirability of resource recovery vs product life extension business models (for example) is fraught. Although the circularity ladder approach provides some insight on this issue, it is unclear to what extent the waste hierarchy ranking of waste management activities reflects environmental impacts higher in the product lifecycle. For example, some LCA studies suggest that reuse may not necessarily be preferable to recycling when the products involved are long lived, have an energy intensive use phase, and are experiencing rapid efficiency improvements.

Fourth, with respect to the product life extension, sharing, and product service system business models, there is a tension between changes in product lifetimes and the diffusion of relatively efficient new product designs. Put differently, this tension reflects a tradeoff between environmental impacts associated with different parts of the product lifecycle. Products that last longer will tend to reduce the extraction and processing of virgin resources (and the associated environmental impacts of these activities), but may also hinder the diffusion of relatively efficient new products. Product category is critical here; this issue is again of most concern for products that are long lived, have an energy intensive use phase, and are experiencing rapid efficiency improvements.

Therefore, while the lifecycle environmental impacts of circular goods and services are mostly significantly smaller than those of linear ones, uncertainty about rebound effects, product innovation and other factors, tend to muddy the picture and prevent from drawing more general conclusions across business models, sectors and product groups. The environmental outcomes of circular business models will therefore need to be carefully assessed on a case by case basis.

Notes

1 Even the resource recovery business model, which upon first inspection is only relevant for the recycling sector, affects a number of extractive sectors via the different materials (metals, paper, plastics, biomass, etc) that it collects and processes.

2 And also relative to other intuitive approaches; some studies use estimates of avoided resource extraction as a proxy for the associated environmental benefits (e.g., Pothen (2017[84]).

3 When assessing the results of "comparative" LCAs, it is also important to keep in mind what the stated counterfactual is. For example, LCAs that focus on processes that extend product lives often assume that the counterfactual is product disposal. In reality, in many cases, not all of the end of life product will be disposed since certain components and materials may be recycled.

4 Further, any such displacement may well take place in jurisdictions other than the one in which the circular business model emerges. For example, if increased secondary metal output in country X leads to reduced domestic demand for primary raw materials, the reduction in resource extraction and processing, and any associated environmental benefits, may take place elsewhere.

5 An additional level of complexity is introduced by the fact that, for some materials, the degree of substitutability declines with each additional material recovery cycle. The static character of LCA makes such effects difficult to incorporate.

6 This is not particularly surprising. It is essentially a restatement of the waste hierarchy concept contained in the European Union's Waste Framework Directive.

7 Defined as total municipal budgetary costs + resource (time) costs incurred by households + external costs associated with landfilling and incineration – (revenues earned from sale of recovered materials + external benefits associated with manufacturing final goods with recycled rather than primary materials less the external costs associated with collecting, transporting, and processing these materials)

8 See Cooper and Gutwoski (2017[130]) for a fuller discussion of these issues in the context of reuse.

9 IDDRI (2014[23]) use the example of cars and refrigerators.

10 As discussed in Section 2.2.3, returning a product to its original condition is central to all definitions of remanufacturing. However, that does not necessarily imply performance levels equal to contemporarily manufactured versions of the same product, even where remanufacturing is complemented with the installation of component upgrades.

11 One complication is that, due to increasingly interconnected global value chains, the upstream and use phase environmental impacts will often emerge in different geographic locations.

12 It has also been suggested that the term "sharing" has positive environmental connotations in and of itself. This is one explanation for why firms not strictly involved in sharing spare capacity seek to label themselves as sharing models (e.g., EU Observer (2017[96]) and European Commission (2016[85])).

13 Any difference in the transport required to use the good is also relevant, but unlikely to be of significant magnitude.

14 As discussed further in Section 4.3.4, one potentially positive implication of increased utilisation and more rapid product turnover is the removal of old, relatively inefficient products from the market.

15 In reality, only a proportion of these hotels would actually have been built in the absence of Airbnb or other sharing platforms. Increased prices resulting from supply shortages would have served to ration some of the excess demand.

16 The authors state that the energy efficiency of typical European and North American residences were compared to those of the most energy efficient hotels (those in the top 5 percentile).

17 Some studies take a different approach. Haefili et al. (2006) ask individuals without access to a car sharing scheme to describe their response to the hypothetical introduction of one. Firnkorn and Muller (2011[102]) ask individuals about their planned response to a recently introduced car sharing scheme.

18 Cervero, Golub and Nee (2007[107]) partially address these concerns by utilising a difference in difference approach. The behaviour of members and non-members is documented at two times: the introduction of a car sharing scheme and five years later. In theory, this allows changes in transport behaviour not associated with car sharing to be isolated.

19 The authors demonstrate this with the example of repaired or refurbished smartphones. According to them, second hand phones are seen as poor substitutes for new phones in developing countries. As such, they are often exported and sold in developing countries where the alternative is no phone at all.

20 Or, as stated by ADEME (2016[92]) in the context of sharing models, “collaborative consumption does not necessarily signify responsible consumption. Indeed, the environmental gain depends strongly on the traditional activity that the collaborative activity replaces”. The potential replacement of public (rather than private) modes of transport by car-pooling and sharing is one such example.

21 To further complicate matters, individual business models do not necessarily operate in isolation, but can interact with each other and, to some extent, become mutually reinforcing.

22 Some of these environmental benefits – particularly those associated with reduced natural resource extraction and processing – will probably accrue in third party jurisdictions (i.e., regions with large extractive sectors).

23 Some business models are probably less susceptible to rebound effects than others. For example, the underlying business case for adopting the classic long life business model is that manufacturers can charge a premium for products that are more durable. As the emergence of the business model is driven primarily by changes in consumer preferences, rather than increasing price competitiveness, there is less potential for rebound effects.

References

ABREE (2016), *Resources and Energy Statistics*, https://industry.gov.au/Office-of-the-Chief-Economist/Publications/Pages/Resources-and-energy-statistics.aspx (accessed on 18 May 2018). [102]

Achterberg, E., J. Hinfelaar and N. Bocken (2016), *The Value Hill Business Model Tool: identifying gaps and opportunities in a circular network*, http://www.scienceandtheenergychallenge.nl/sites/default/files/multimedia/organization/sec/2016-06-16_NWO_Sc4CE/NWO%20Sc4CE%20-%20Workshop%20Business%20Models%20-%20Paper%20on%20Circular%20Business%20Models.pdf (accessed on 13 September 2018). [75]

ADEME (2016), *Potentiels d'expansion de la consommation collaborative pour réduire les impacts environnemenaux*, https://www.ademe.fr/potentiels-dexpansion-consommation-collaborative-reduire-impacts-environnementaux (accessed on 14 September 2018). [39]

Agrawal, V., A. Atasu and K. van Ittersum (2015), "Remanufacturing, Third-Party Competition, and Consumers' Perceived Value of New Products", *Management Science*, Vol. 61/1, pp. 60-72, http://dx.doi.org/10.1287/mnsc.2014.2099. [109]

Agrawal, V. et al. (2012), "Is Leasing Greener Than Selling?", *Management Science*, Vol. 58/3, pp. 523-533, http://dx.doi.org/10.1287/mnsc.1110.1428. [44]

AirBnb (2018), *Night Limits: Frequently Asked Questions*, https://www.airbnb.com/help/article/1628/night-limits--frequently-asked-questions (accessed on 13 September 2018). [112]

AmCham (2017), *China (Ningbo) Remanufacturing Industry International Cooperation Forum*, https://www.amcham-shanghai.org/en/article/china-ningbo-remanufacturing-industry-international-cooperation-forum-0?lang=en (accessed on 13 September 2018). [105]

Ashman (2017), *The Internet of Things: paving the way for renewable energy? – Capgemini Worldwide*, https://www.capgemini.com/2017/08/the-internet-of-things-paving-the-way-for-renewable-energy/ (accessed on 13 September 2018). [132]

Astrup, T. et al. (2015), "Life cycle assessment of thermal Waste-to-Energy technologies: Review and recommendations", *Waste Management*, Vol. 37, pp. 104-115, http://dx.doi.org/10.1016/j.wasman.2014.06.011. [16]

BBC (2017), *Beijing bans new bikes as sharing schemes cause chaos - BBC News*, https://www.bbc.com/news/business-41197341 (accessed on 13 September 2018). [122]

Bernardo, C., C. Simões and L. Pinto (2016), "Environmental and economic life cycle analysis of plastic waste management options. A review Cost management for waste to energy systems using life cycle costing approach: A case study from Environmental and Economic Life Cycle Analysis of Plastic Waste Management Options. A Review", *China Journal of Renewable and Sustainable Energy*, Vol. 10/123, pp. 140001-140002, http://dx.doi.org/10.1063/1.4958429. [6]

BIR (2008), *Report on the Environmental Benefits of Recycling*, http://www.mgg-recycling.com/wp-content/uploads/2013/06/BIR_CO2_report.pdf (accessed on 14 September 2018). [4]

Biswas, W. and M. Rosano (2011), "A life cycle greenhouse gas assessment of remanufactured refrigeration and air conditioning compressors", *International Journal of Sustainable Manufacturing*, Vol. 2/2/3, p. 222, http://dx.doi.org/10.1504/IJSM.2011.042153. [28]

Bocken, N. et al. (2016), "Product design and business model strategies for a circular economy", *Journal of Industrial and Production Engineering*, Vol. 33/5, pp. 308-320, http://dx.doi.org/10.1080/21681015.2016.1172124. [85]

Böcker, L. and T. Meelen (2017), "Sharing for people, planet or profit? Analysing motivations for intended sharing economy participation", *Environmental Innovation and Societal Transitions*, Vol. 23, pp. 28-39, http://dx.doi.org/10.1016/J.EIST.2016.09.004. [35]

CDP (2016), *Embedding a carbon price into business strategy*, https://b8f65cb373b1b7b15feb-c70d8ead6ced550b4d987d7c03fcdd1d.ssl.cf3.rackcdn.com/cms/reports/documents/000/001/132/original/CDP_Carbon_Price_report_2016.pdf?1474899276 (accessed on 13 September 2018). [95]

Cervero, R., A. Golub and B. Nee (2007), "City CarShare: longer-term travel demand and car ownership impacts", *Transportation Research Record: Journal of the Transportation Research Board* 1992, pp. 70-80. [53]

Chen, T. and K. Kockelman (2016), "Carsharing's life-cycle impacts on energy use and greenhouse gas emissions", *Transportation Research Part D: Transport and Environment*, Vol. 47, pp. 276-284, http://dx.doi.org/10.1016/j.trd.2016.05.012. [60]

Cleantech (2014), *Airbnb says it's better for the environment than hotels*, https://venturebeat.com/2014/07/31/airbnb-says-its-better-for-the-environment-than-hotels/ (accessed on 14 September 2018). [43]

Cleary, J. (2009), "Life cycle assessments of municipal solid waste management systems: A comparative analysis of selected peer-reviewed literature", *Environment International*, Vol. 35/8, pp. 1256-1266, http://dx.doi.org/10.1016/J.ENVINT.2009.07.009. [14]

Climate Home (2016), *Exxon, Shell, Total, Statoil renew clean energy drive*, http://www.climatechangenews.com/2016/05/23/exxon-shell-total-and-statoil-make-clean-energy-plays/ (accessed on 13 September 2018). [96]

Cooper, T. (2004), "Inadequate Life?Evidence of Consumer Attitudes to Product Obsolescence", *Journal of Consumer Policy*, Vol. 27/4, pp. 421-449, http://dx.doi.org/10.1007/s10603-004-2284-6. [83]

COWI (2008), *Promoting Innovative Business Models with Environmental Benefits*, http://www.cowi.com (accessed on 13 September 2018). [93]

De Groene, Z. and Ethica (2015), *Boosting Circular Design for a Circular Economy*, http://degroenezaak.com/wp-content/uploads/2015/03/Boosting_Circular_Design_for_a_Circular_Economy_FINAL.pdf (accessed on 14 September 2018). [2]

DEFRA (2011), "Longer Product Lifetimes: Life Cycle Impact of Nine Products", http://sciencesearch.defra.gov.uk/Default.aspx?Menu=Menu&Module=More&Location=None&Completed=0&ProjectID=17047 (accessed on 14 September 2018). [20]

Dimitropoulos, J. (2007), "Energy productivity improvements and the rebound effect: An overview of the state of knowledge", *Energy Policy*, Vol. 35/12, pp. 6354-6363, http://dx.doi.org/10.1016/J.ENPOL.2007.07.028. [69]

Doka, G. and S. Ziegler (2001), *Complete Life Cycle Assessment for Vehicle Models of the Mobility CarSharing Fleet Switzerland*, http://www.doka.ch/DokaMobilitySTRCproc01.pdf (accessed on 17 September 2018). [49]

DSEWPC (2012), *The Australian Recycling Sector Report*, https://www.environment.gov.au/system/files/resources/dc87fd71-6bcb-4135-b916-71dd349fc0b8/files/australian-recycling-sector.pdf (accessed on 14 September 2018). [12]

EEA (2006), "Paper and cardboard — recovery or disposal? Review of life cycle assessment and cost-benefit analysis on the recovery and disposal of paper and cardboard", http://www.pedz.uni-mannheim.de/daten/edz-bn/eua/06/technical_rep_5_2006.pdf (accessed on 14 September 2018). [7]

Ekvall, T. et al. (2007), *Limitations and amendments in life-cycle assessment on waste management*, https://www.researchgate.net/publication/255823714_Limitations_and_amendments_in_life-cycle_assessment_on_waste_management (accessed on 14 September 2018). [18]

Ellen Macarthur Foundation (2013), *Towards the Circular Economy*, https://www.ellenmacarthurfoundation.org/assets/downloads/publications/Ellen-MacArthur-Foundation-Towards-the-Circular-Economy-vol.1.pdf (accessed on 17 September 2018). [64]

Ellen McArthur Foundation (2018), *Eleven companies take major step towards a New Plastics Economy*, https://www.ellenmacarthurfoundation.org/news/11-companies-take-major-step-towards-a-new-plastics-economy (accessed on 13 September 2018). [99]

Ellen McArthur Foundation (2015), *GROWTH WITHIN: A CIRCULAR ECONOMY VISION FOR A COMPETITIVE EUROPE*, https://www.ellenmacarthurfoundation.org/assets/downloads/publications/EllenMacArthurFoundation_Growth-Within_July15.pdf (accessed on 13 September 2018). [89]

ERN (2015), *Remanufacturing Market Study*, European Remanufacturing Network, http://www.remanufacturing.eu/assets/pdfs/remanufacturing-market-study.pdf. [31]

European Commission (2018), *Plastic Waste: a European strategy to protect the planet, defend our citizens and empower our industries*, http://europa.eu/rapid/press-release_IP-18-5_en.htm (accessed on 18 January 2018). [97]

European Commission (2016), *Scoping the Sharing Economy: Origins, Definitions, Impact and Regulatory Issues*, https://ec.europa.eu/jrc (accessed on 14 September 2018). [37]

European Commission (2016), *Study on socioeconomic impacts of increased reparability of increased reparability - EU Law and Publications*, https://publications.europa.eu/en/publication-detail/-/publication/c6865b39-2628-11e6-86d0-01aa75ed71a1 (accessed on 13 September 2018). [128]

Eurostat (2018), *Eurostat - Trade in recyclable raw materials*, http://ec.europa.eu/eurostat/tgm/table.do?tab=table&plugin=1&language=en&pcode=cei_srm020 (accessed on 28 March 2018). [123]

Firnkorn, J. and M. Müller (2011), "What will be the environmental effects of new free-floating car-sharing systems? The case of car2go in Ulm", *Ecological Economics*, Vol. 70/8, pp. 1519-1528, http://dx.doi.org/10.1016/J.ECOLECON.2011.03.014. [57]

Frenken, K. and J. Schor (2017), "Putting the sharing economy into perspective", *Environmental Innovation and Societal Transitions*, Vol. 23, pp. 3-10, http://dx.doi.org/10.1016/J.EIST.2017.01.003. [33]

Gaillochet, C. and P. Chalmin (2009), *From waste to ressources : world waste survey 2009*, https://www.researchgate.net/publication/41222409_From_waste_to_ressources_world_waste_survey_2009 (accessed on 13 September 2018). [80]

Gao, W. et al. (2017), "Investigation on the Comparative Life Cycle Assessment between Newly Manufacturing and Remanufacturing Turbochargers", *Procedia CIRP*, Vol. 61, pp. 750-755, http://dx.doi.org/10.1016/j.procir.2016.11.214. [32]

Geyer, R., J. Jambeck and K. Law (2017), "Production, use, and fate of all plastics ever made", *Science Advances*, Vol. 3/7, p. e1700782, http://dx.doi.org/10.1126/sciadv.1700782. [124]

Gutowski, T. et al. (2011), "Remanufacturing and Energy Savings", *Environmental Science & Technology*, Vol. 45/10, pp. 4540-4547, http://dx.doi.org/10.1021/es102598b. [26]

Hertwich, E. (2005), *Consumption and the Rebound Effect An Industrial Ecology Perspective*, http://mitpress.mit.edu/jie (accessed on 17 September 2018). [66]

HPRC (2015), *Environmental Impacts of Recycling Compared to Other Waste Disposal Methods*, https://docs.wixstatic.com/ugd/49d7a0_6bb3ebb481ec49ceafef92f0b0ba010d.pdf (accessed on 28 March 2018). [5]

IDDRI (2014), *The sharing economy: make it sustainable*, http://www.iddri.org (accessed on 13 September 2018). [36]

IMSA (2015), *Circular business models: an introduction to IMSA's circular business model scan*, https://groenomstilling.erhvervsstyrelsen.dk/sites/default/files/media/imsa_circular_business_models_-_april_2015_-_part_1.pdf (accessed on 13 September 2018). [76]

Intlekofer, K., B. Bras and M. Ferguson (2010), "Energy Implications of Product Leasing", http://dx.doi.org/10.1021/es9036836. [48]

Jagtap, S. (2017), *IoT Concepts for Improving the Resource Efficiency of Food Supply Chains*, http://www.manufacturingfoodfutures.com/documents/utilization-of-internet-of-things-concepts-to-improve-resource-efficiency-of-food-supply-chains-sandeep-jagtap.pdf (accessed on 13 September 2018). [131]

Kara, H. (2010), *Comparative Carbon Footprint Analysis of New and Remanufactured Inkjet Cartridges*, Centre for Remanufacturing and Reuse (CPR), http://ww.ebpgroup.com/wp-content/uploads/pdf/CCFreport.pdf (accessed on 19 October 2018). [25]

Kerr, W. and C. Ryan (2001), "Eco-efficiency gains from remanufacturing", *Journal of Cleaner Production*, Vol. 9/1, pp. 75-81, http://dx.doi.org/10.1016/S0959-6526(00)00032-9. [21]

Kinnaman, T., T. Shinkuma and M. Yamamoto (2014), "The socially optimal recycling rate: Evidence from Japan", *Journal of Environmental Economics and Management*, Vol. 68, pp. 54-70, http://dx.doi.org/10.1016/j.jeem.2014.01.004. [19]

Koesler, S., K. Swales and K. Turner (2016), "International spillover and rebound effects from increased energy efficiency in Germany", *Energy Economics*, Vol. 54, pp. 444-452, http://dx.doi.org/10.1016/J.ENECO.2015.12.011. [70]

Koffler, C. et al. (2013), "Tackling the Downcycling Issue—A Revised Approach to Value-Corrected Substitution in Life Cycle Assessment of Aluminum", *Sustainability*, Vol. 5/11, pp. 4546-4560, http://dx.doi.org/10.3390/su5114546. [65]

Kuo, T. (2011), "Simulation of purchase or rental decision-making based on product service system", *The International Journal of Advanced Manufacturing Technology*, Vol. 52/9-12, pp. 1239-1249, http://dx.doi.org/10.1007/s00170-010-2768-2. [45]

Lacy, P. and J. Rutqvist (2015), *Waste to wealth : the circular economy advantage.* [78]

Lane, C. (2005), "PhillyCarShare: First-Year Social and Mobility Impacts of Carsharing in Philadelphia, Pennsylvania", *Transportation Research Record: Journal of the Transportation Research Board*, Vol. 1927, pp. 158-166, http://dx.doi.org/10.3141/1927-18. [50]

Laurent, A. et al. (2014), "Review of LCA studies of solid waste management systems – Part I: Lessons learned and perspectives", *Waste Management*, Vol. 34/3, pp. 573-588, http://dx.doi.org/10.1016/J.WASMAN.2013.10.045. [13]

Lavery, G. et al. (2013), *The Next Manufacturing Revolution*, http://www.2degreesnetwork.com (accessed on 13 September 2018). [108]

Le Moigne, R. and L. Georgeault (2016), "Remanufacturing: Une Formidable Opportunité Pour La France Industrielle de Demain", https://www.wmaker.net/eco-circulaire/attachment/656994/ (accessed on 13 September 2018). [88]

Lewandowski, M. (2016), "Designing the Business Models for Circular Economy—Towards the Conceptual Framework", *Sustainability*, Vol. 8/1, p. 43, http://dx.doi.org/10.3390/su8010043. [77]

Liu, Z. et al. (2014), "Life Cycle Assessment-based Comparative Evaluation of Originally Manufactured and Remanufactured Diesel Engines", *Journal of Industrial Ecology*, Vol. 18/4, pp. 567-576, http://dx.doi.org/10.1111/jiec.12137. [29]

Long, X. et al. (2017), "Strategy Analysis of Recycling and Remanufacturing by Remanufacturers in Closed-Loop Supply Chain", *Sustainability*, Vol. 9/10, pp. 1-29, https://ideas.repec.org/a/gam/jsusta/v9y2017i10p1818-d114402.html (accessed on 13 September 2018). [82]

Martin, E. and S. Shaheen (2011), "Greenhouse Gas Emission Impacts of Carsharing in North America", *IEEE Transactions on Intelligent Transportation Systems*, Vol. 12/4, pp. 1074-1086, http://dx.doi.org/10.1109/TITS.2011.2158539. [56]

Martin, E., S. Shaheen and J. Lidicker (2011), "Impact of Carsharing on Household Vehicle Holdings", http://dx.doi.org/10.3141/2143-19. [55]

McCarthy, A., R. Dellink and R. Bibas (2018), "The Macroeconomics of the Circular Economy Transition: A Critical Review of Modelling Approaches", *OECD Environment Working Papers*, No. 130, OECD Publishing, Paris, http://dx.doi.org/10.1787/af983f9a-en. [68]

Millard-Ball, A. et al. (2005), *Car-Sharing: Where and How It Succeeds*, https://www.nap.edu/download/13559 (accessed on 17 September 2018). [51]

MOMO (2010), *The State of European Car-Sharing*, http://www.eltis.org/sites/default/files/tool/the_state_of_carsharing_europe.pdf (accessed on 18 October 2018). [54]

Morris, J., H. Matthews and C. Morawski (2012), "Review and meta-analysis of 82 studies on end-of-life management methods for source separated organics", *Waste Management*, Vol. 33/3, pp. 545-551, http://dx.doi.org/10.1016/J.WASMAN.2012.08.004. [9]

Navigant Research (2015), *Carsharing Programs*, https://www.navigantresearch.com/reports/carsharing-programs (accessed on 13 September 2018). [120]

NCASI (2012), *Summary of the Literature on the Treatment of Paper and Paper Packaging Products*, https://twosidesna.org/US/NCASI-Summary-of-the-Literature-on-the-Treatment-of-Paper-and-Paper-Packaging-Products-Recycling-in-Life-Cycle-Assessment-2011/ (accessed on 14 September 2018). [8]

Neto, J. and J. Bloemhof-Ruwaard (2009), *The Environmental Gains of Remanufacturing: Evidence from the Computer and Mobile Industry*, ERIM Report Series Reference No. ERS-2009-024-LIS, https://ssrn.com/abstract=1410467 (accessed on 19 October 2018). [24]

Nijland, H. and J. Van Meerkerk (2017), "Mobility and environmental impacts of car sharing in the Netherlands", *Environmental Innovation and Societal Transitions*, Vol. 23, pp. 84-91, http://dx.doi.org/10.1016/j.eist.2017.02.001. [61]

Nordic Council of Ministers, T. (2017), *Environmental impacts and potential of the sharing economy*, TemaNord, Nordic Council of Ministers, Copenhagen K, http://dx.doi.org/10.6027/TN2017-554. [41]

NSW EPA (2010), *Environmental benefits of recycling*, https://www.epa.nsw.gov.au/publications/recyclereuse/100058-benefits-of-recycling (accessed on 18 September 2018). [17]

OECD (2018), *ONLINE PLATFORMS: A PRACTICAL APPROACH TO THEIR ECONOMIC AND SOCIAL IMPACTS*, https://one.oecd.org/document/DSTI/CDEP(2018)5/en/pdf (accessed on 13 September 2018). [116]

OECD (2017), *Economic Features of Chemical Leasing*, https://one.oecd.org/document/ENV/JM/MONO(2017)10/en/pdf (accessed on 13 September 2018). [47]

OECD (2017), *MAPPING SUPPORT FOR PRIMARY AND SECONDARY METAL PRODUCTION*, https://one.oecd.org/document/ENV/EPOC/WPRPW(2016)2/FINAL/en/pdf (accessed on 13 September 2018). [103]

OECD (2017), *THE POSSIBLE ROLE OF DIGITAL PLATFORMS IN THE COLLECTION OF VAT/GST ON ONLINE SALES*, https://one.oecd.org/document/CTPA/CFA/WP9(2017)6/en/pdf (accessed on 13 September 2018). [115]

OECD (2016), *PROTECTING CONSUMERS IN PEER PLATFORM MARKETS: EXPLORING THE ISSUES*, https://one.oecd.org/document/DSTI/CP(2015)4/REV2/en/pdf (accessed on 13 September 2018). [117]

OECD (2012), *OECD Environmental Outlook to 2050: The Consequences of Inaction*, OECD Publishing, Paris, http://dx.doi.org/10.1787/9789264122246-en. [72]

OICA (2015), *Vehicles in use*, http://www.oica.net/category/vehicles-in-use/ (accessed on 13 September 2018). [119]

Osterwalder, A., Y. Pigneur and C. Tucci (2010), *Clarifying Business Models: Origins, Present, and Future of the Concept*, https://www.researchgate.net/publication/37426694_Clarifying_Business_Models_Origins_Present_and_Future_of_the_Concept (accessed on 13 September 2018). [74]

Parker, D. et al. (2015), *Remanufacturing Market Study*, http://www.remanufacturing.eu/assets/pdfs/remanufacturing-market-study.pdf (accessed on 13 September 2018). [87]

Parrado, R., F. Eni and E. Mattei (2017), *The Economy-Wide Rebound Effect and Climate Policy Effectiveness in a Multiregional General Equilibrium Framework*, https://www.gtap.agecon.purdue.edu/resources/download/6853.pdf (accessed on 17 September 2018). [71]

PWC (2015), *The sharing economy*, https://www.pwc.com/us/en/services/consulting/library/consumer-intelligence-series/sharing-economy.html (accessed on 14 September 2018). [34]

Recode (2017), *Airbnb is on track to rack up more than 100 million stays this year — and that's only the beginning of its threat to the hotel industry - Recode*, https://www.recode.net/2017/7/19/15949782/airbnb-100-million-stays-2017-threat-business-hotel-industry (accessed on 28 August 2018). [111]

Ryden, C. and E. Morin (2005), "Mobility services for urban sustainability: Environmental assessment", *Moses Report WP6, Trivector Traffic AB, Stockholm, Sweden*. [52]

San Francisco Business Portal (2018), *Short-Term Rental*, https://businessportal.sfgov.org/start/starter-kits/short-term-rental (accessed on 13 September 2018). [113]

SEI (2005), *Rethinking the Waste Hierarchy*, http://www.imv.dk (accessed on 14 September 2018). [1]

Shaheen, S. and A. Cohen (2016), *Innovative Mobility Carsharing Outlook*, https://cloudfront.escholarship.org/dist/prd/content/qt49j961wb/qt49j961wb.pdf?t=pa6fa3&v=lg (accessed on 13 September 2018). [118]

Shaheen, S. and E. Martin (2016), *Impacts of car2go on Vehicle Ownership, Modal Shift, Vehicle Miles Traveled, and Greenhouse Gas Emissions*, Transportation Sustainability Research Center, UC Berkeley, http://www.tsrc.berkeley.edu (accessed on 18 October 2018). [59]

Sierra Club (2017), *Is the Sharing Economy Truly Green?*, https://www.sierraclub.org/sierra/2016-2-march-april/green-life/sharing-economy-truly-green (accessed on 14 September 2018). [38]

Smith, V. and G. Keoleian (2004), "The Value of Remanufactured Engines: Life-Cycle Environmental and Economic Perspectives", *Journal of Industrial Ecology*, Vol. 8/1-2, pp. 193-221, http://dx.doi.org/10.1162/1088198041269463. [22]

Sorrell, S. and J. Dimitropoulos (2008), "The rebound effect: Microeconomic definitions, limitations and extensions", *Ecological Economics*, Vol. 65/3, pp. 636-649, http://dx.doi.org/10.1016/J.ECOLECON.2007.08.013. [67]

Spelman, C. and B. Sheerman (2014), *Triple Win: The Social, Economic, and Environmental Case for Remanufacturing*, http://www.policyconnect.org.uk/apmg (accessed on 13 September 2018). [86]

Stasko, T., A. Buck and H. Oliver Gao (2013), "Carsharing in a university setting: Impacts on [58]
vehicle ownership, parking demand, and mobility in Ithaca, NY", *Transport Policy*, Vol. 30, pp. 262-268, http://dx.doi.org/10.1016/j.tranpol.2013.09.018.

Statista (2017), *Airbnb - Statistics & Facts*, https://www.statista.com/topics/2273/airbnb/ [91]
(accessed on 13 September 2018).

Steinhilper, R. (1998), *Remanufacturing: The Ultimate Form of Recycling Fraunhofer IRB [23]
Verlag*, Fraunhofer IRB Verlag, http://www.elitecreativesolutions.com/files/steinhilper_part1.pdf (accessed on 19 October 2018).

STR (2017), *Airbnb & Hotel Performance*, [90]
http://www.str.com/Media/Default/Research/STR_AirbnbHotelPerformance.pdf (accessed on 13 September 2018).

Stuart, E., C. Goldman and D. Gilligan (2014), *The U.S. ESCO Industry: Recent Trends, Current [130]
Size and Remaining Market Potential*, http://aceee.org/files/proceedings/2014/data/papers/3-319.pdf (accessed on 13 September 2018).

Taranic, I., A. Behrens and C. Topi (2016), *Understanding the Circular Economy in Europe, [81]
from Resource Efficiency to Sharing Platforms: The CEPS Framework*, http://www.ceps.eu (accessed on 13 September 2018).

Tech Crunch (2015), *Upgrades Fueling Second Hand Smartphone Sales Boom, Says Gartner | [126]
TechCrunch*, https://techcrunch.com/2015/02/18/reuse-dont-recycle/?guccounter=1 (accessed on 13 September 2018).

The Guardian (2017), *'Screen fatigue' sees UK ebook sales plunge 17% as readers return to [129]
print | Books | The Guardian*, https://www.theguardian.com/books/2017/apr/27/screen-fatigue-sees-uk-ebook-sales-plunge-17-as-readers-return-to-print (accessed on 13 September 2018).

The Herald (2017), *Major blow for Airbnb users: New law to restrict New York City apartment [114]
rentals | Newcastle Herald*, https://www.theherald.com.au/story/4444330/major-blow-for-airbnb-users-new-law-to-restrict-new-york-city-apartment-rentals/?cs=34 (accessed on 13 September 2018).

Thompson, A. et al. (2010), *Benefits of a Product Service System Approach for Long-life [79]
Products: The Case of Light Tubes*, http://www.ep.liu.se/ecp/077/011/ecp10077011.pdf (accessed on 13 September 2018).

TNO (2013), *Opportunities for a circular economy in the Netherlands (translated from: Kansen [63]
voor een circulaire economie in Nederland)*, https://www.rijksoverheid.nl/documenten/rapporten/2013/06/20/tno-rapport-kansen-voor-de-circulaire-economie-in-nederland.

Travel Weekly (2016), *Airbnb vs. the hotel industry*, https://www.travelweekly.com/Danny- [110]
King/Airbnb-vs-hotel-industry (accessed on 13 September 2018).

Trend Force (2017), *Global Smartphone Production Volume Totaled 1.36 Billion Units; Samsung Held On as Leader While OPPO and Vivo Burst into Global Top Five*, https://press.trendforce.com/node/view/2741.html (accessed on 13 September 2018). [127]

Trinomics (2017), *What is the environmental impact of the sharing economy?*, http://trinomics.eu/sharing-economy/ (accessed on 14 September 2018). [40]

Tukker, A. (2015), "Product services for a resource-efficient and circular economy – a review", *Journal of Cleaner Production*, Vol. 97, pp. 76-91, http://dx.doi.org/10.1016/J.JCLEPRO.2013.11.049. [46]

Tukker, A. (2004), "Eight types of product–service system: eight ways to sustainability? Experiences from SusProNet", *Business Strategy and the Environment*, Vol. 13/4, pp. 246-260, http://dx.doi.org/10.1002/bse.414. [92]

UN Combrade (2018), *UN Comtrade | International Trade Statistics Database*, https://comtrade.un.org/ (accessed on 05 June 2018). [104]

UNEP (2017), "RESOURCE EFFICIENCY: POTENTIAL AND ECONOMIC IMPLICATIONS", http://www.resourcepanel.org/sites/default/files/documents/document/media/resource_efficiency_report_march_2017_web_res.pdf (accessed on 23 April 2018). [73]

UNEP (2013), *Metal Recycling – Opportunitites, Limits, Infrastructure (Full report)*, United Nations Environment Programme, http://www.resourcepanel.org/sites/default/files/documents/document/media/e-book_metals_report2b_recyclingopportunities_130919.pdf (accessed on 18 May 2018). [100]

US EPA (2017), "U.S. EPA Sustainable Materials Management Program Strategic Plan", https://www.epa.gov/sites/production/files/2016-03/documents/smm_strategic_plan_october_2015.pdf (accessed on 23 April 2018). [94]

US ITC (2012), *Remanufactured Goods: An Overview of the U.S. and Global Industries, Markets, and Trade*, http://www.usitc.gov (accessed on 13 September 2018). [106]

USGS (2016), *USGS Minerals Information: Commodity Statistics and Information*, https://minerals.usgs.gov/minerals/pubs/commodity/ (accessed on 18 May 2018). [98]

Valerio, F. (2010), *Environmental Impacts of Post-Consumer Material Managements: recycling, biological treatments, incineration*, http://www.federico-valerio.it/wp-content/uploads/2014/01/MPC-environ-impact.pdf (accessed on 14 September 2018). [11]

Van Ewijk, S., J. Stegemann and P. Ekins (2017), "Global Life Cycle Paper Flows, Recycling Metrics, and Material Efficiency", *Journal of Industrial Ecology*, http://dx.doi.org/10.1111/jiec.12613. [125]

Wang, Y. (2016), *Remanufacturing Mission to China*, https://connect.innovateuk.org/web/remanufacturing/article-view/-/blogs/new-remanufacturing-standards- (accessed on 13 September 2018). [107]

Warsen, J., M. Laumer and W. Momberg (2011), "Comparative Life Cycle Assessment of Remanufacturing and New Manufacturing of a Manual Transmission", in *Glocalized Solutions for Sustainability in Manufacturing*, Springer Berlin Heidelberg, Berlin, Heidelberg, http://dx.doi.org/10.1007/978-3-642-19692-8_12. [27]

WEF (2016), *Understanding the Sharing Economy*, http://www3.weforum.org/docs/WEF_Understanding_the_Sharing_Economy_report_2016.pdf (accessed on 14 September 2018). [42]

WEF (2016), *Understanding the Sharing Economy*, http://www3.weforum.org/docs/WEF_Understanding_the_Sharing_Economy_report_2016.pdf (accessed on 13 September 2018). [133]

Wilson, J. et al. (2014), "Remanufacturing of turbine blades by laser direct deposition with its energy and environmental impact analysis", *Journal of Cleaner Production*, Vol. 80, pp. 170-178, http://dx.doi.org/10.1016/j.jclepro.2014.05.084. [30]

World Steel (2016), *Crude Steel Production*, https://www.worldsteel.org/statistics/statistics-archive/steel-archive.html. [101]

WRAP (2011), *Realising the Reuse Value of Household WEEE*, http://www.wrap.org.uk (accessed on 13 September 2018). [84]

WRAP (2010), *Environmental benefits of recycling*, http://www.wrap.org.uk (accessed on 14 September 2018). [3]

WRAP (2010), "Environmental benefits of recycling – 2010 update 1", http://www.wrap.org.uk/sites/files/wrap/Environmental_benefits_of_recycling_2010_update.3b174d59.8816.pdf (accessed on 28 March 2018). [10]

WRAP (2006), *Environmental benefits of recycling*, https://cri.dk/sites/cri.dk/files/dokumenter/artikler/filef7e8.pdf (accessed on 14 September 2018). [15]

WRI (2015), *Carsharing: A Vehicle for Sustainable Mobility in Emerging Markets*, http://wrirosscities.org/sites/default/files/WRI_Carsharing_Vehicle_Sustainable_Mobility_Emerging_Markets.pdf (accessed on 13 September 2018). [121]

Zink, T. and R. Geyer (2017), "Circular Economy Rebound", *Journal of Industrial Ecology*, Vol. 21/3, pp. 593-602, http://dx.doi.org/10.1111/jiec.12545. [62]

Chapter 5. Policy Implications

This chapter offers a summary of the policy implications that emerge from this report. The discussion is intended to provide a set of high level policy principles rather than specific guidance for individual business models. Thus, the factors that serve to hinder the general adoption of circular business models are identified, and the set of policy approaches that could address them discussed. Developing more specific policy guidance would require more detailed analysis of a particular business model within individual sectors: this could be considered for future work.

5.1. The findings of this report

Circular business models – those that serve to reduce the extraction and use of natural resources and the generation of industrial and consumer wastes – operate in a number of economic sectors. Because these business models use already existing materials and products as inputs, their environmental footprint tends to be considerably smaller than that for traditional business models. This idea is supported by the life cycle analysis literature, where it has been demonstrated that secondary raw materials, repaired and remanufactured products, and shared assets typically have relatively small global warming, acidification, and toxicity potential. As such, the continued adoption of circular modes of production, to the extent that it displaces production from traditional modes (and notwithstanding any associated rebound effects) could have important first order environmental benefits.

The market penetration of circular business models remains limited. The most successful circular mode of production – producing secondary raw materials from waste – only accounts for 30 to 40% of the physical output of the sectors that it is best established in (pulp and paper and steel). Other forms of circular production – refurbishment and remanufacturing, the sharing of spare capacity, and the provision of services rather than products – continue to represent a small fraction of overall output (either in physical or economic terms). Although it is clear that some of these business models have experienced rapid recent growth, much of this has been confined to a handful of economic niches. Sharing models in the accommodation sector or product service systems in the transport sector are frequently cited examples. Transitioning to a more circular and resource efficient economy – one where the environmental impacts associated with economic production and consumption are significantly reduced – will require much more widespread penetration of these business models. Policy can play an important role in this respect.

5.2. The role of policy

5.2.1. General considerations

This section offers an initial discussion on how policy can help to promote the broader adoption of circular business models. The discussion is intended to provide a set of high level policy principles rather than specific guidance for individual business models. The reason is twofold. First, not all circular business models are created equal; it is not entirely clear which have the greatest scalability and environmental potential. As such, it may be prudent to avoid targeting policies at specific business models, and instead focus on implementing a policy framework that provides coherent incentives for closing and slowing resource loops, and narrowing resource flows throughout the economy.

Second, the barriers that hinder the emergence of these business models vary widely according to the business model considered and the sectors they are applied in. It is beyond the scope of this report to consider all possible permutations; developing more operational policy guidance would require deeper analysis for specific business models and sectors. The application of PSS models in two contrasting sectors (urban mobility and chemicals) serves to illustrate this. In the former case, the majority of transactions are of a B2C nature; the continued adoption of urban car sharing will be driven largely by the convenience of sharing and by underlying consumer attitudes towards car ownership. Urban transport policy will be a key factor for both. In the case of chemical leasing, where the majority of transactions are of a B2B nature, more widespread uptake will largely depend on underlying commercial considerations. The stringency of chemicals policy is therefore likely to be a key driver (OECD, 2017[1]).

5.2.2. Common barriers to circular business model adoption and potential policy responses

There are various reasons why the market share of circular business models may be sub-optimal. One shared characteristic of these business models is that they use virgin resources and environmental goods less intensively than the traditional businesses that they compete against. These inputs are cheaper than they would be if the externalities – the environmental damages – resulting from their use were addressed. This probably serves to provide traditional business models with a competitive advantage. *Policy can help to ensure that the full environmental costs of production and consumption activities are reflected in market prices.*

Another characteristic of many circular business models, particularly the circular supply, resource recovery and product life extension business models, is the need for collaboration within and across value chains. Externalities resulting from design decisions made by traditional manufacturing firms have implications for the feasibility of material recovery and product life extension activities further downstream. Similarly, the existence of search and transaction costs can make it difficult for industrial symbiosis to emerge across sectors. *Policy can help to improve collaboration within and across sectoral value chains. Fostering industrial symbiosis clusters, promoting online material marketplaces, establishing secondary raw material certification schemes, and, more generally, facilitation of cooperation within and across value chains may be worthwhile initial steps.*

Policy misalignments are sometimes also hindering the emergence of circular business models. One example concerns the provision of subsidies to extractive and material processing sectors, which can extend into the billions of dollars for fossil fuels (OECD, 2015[2]), metals (OECD, 2017[3]), fisheries (OECD, 2018[4]), and agriculture (OECD, 2016[5]). Another example concerns the tendency to tax labour inputs at significantly higher rates than capital and natural resource inputs. A recent Club of Rome report on the circular economy (Wijkman, Skånberg and Berglund, 2016[6]) states that, "modern tax systems in the EU apply high rates to employment while leaving the use of natural resources tax-free or even subsidized". For the same reason as that outlined above, these policies probably serve to favour traditional modes of economic production. *Policy makers could therefore consider what objectives existing fiscal policy is serving, and whether a fiscal realignment could lead to improved environmental and equity outcomes.*

There are also a variety of status quo biases that effectively lend inertia to current patterns of economic development, often at the expense of the emergence of circular business models. One example concerns the elevated price volatility that is present in secondary materials markets. This volatility – which is itself a product of limited market development – probably dis-incentivises investment in new secondary production capacity. Another example concerns the various trade regulations that serve to limit cross border flows of secondary materials and used products (OECD, 2018[7]). While many of these restrictions serve a clear purpose within a linear economic system, they may hinder the development of the reverse logistics that are central to some circular business models. A final example relates to the regulatory exceptions that are often granted to heavily polluting or incumbent firms, thereby hindering the entry of firms with more circular business models.[1] *Policy could therefore aim to ensure that existing regulatory frameworks are coherent and fit for purpose, and not serving to preserve an existing status quo.*

Another major challenge concerning status quo bias relates to consumer behaviour. In some cases, the development of markets for circular products and services appears to be held back by a lack of consumer interest. For example, in most consumer goods sectors, there are only a small number of manufacturers that attempt to differentiate themselves by marketing long lived, but relatively expensive products (the clothing manufacturer Patagonia is one such example). Despite the fact that higher quality products may be cost competitive when considered over their useful life, many consumers prefer to opt for low quality substitutes.[2] *Policy makers could therefore consider how existing educational and information programs can be improved to provide individuals with a better understanding of the unintended consequences of their consumption choices. The use of behavioural insights and nudges, such as through labelling requirements, may be a promising way forward.*

Policy makers interested in promoting the more widespread adoption of circular business models could, in addition to addressing the issues highlighted above, implement a range of additional enabling policy measures. These policies will clearly differ according to the business model concerned, but can be thought of generally as promoting either the supply of circular products ("supply-push measures") or demand for them ("demand-pull measures"). *Examples of the former include eco-design standards, strengthened EPR schemes, and the provision of targeted R&D funding. Examples of the latter include differentiated VAT rates, recycled content mandates, product labelling standards, and green public procurement.*

Finally, one issue highlighted in this review is the importance of rebound effects, whereby initial reductions in resource extraction and use are partially offset via various indirect economic feedbacks. Any future transition to a more resource efficient and circular economy will be at least partially driven by the diffusion of material efficient production technologies and the emergence of more cost competitive circular business models. The resulting reduction in price levels is likely to trigger a rebound effect as consumers allocate the associated savings to additional consumption, and manufacturers substitute towards inputs that have become relatively cheap (probably including natural resources). There is little that policy makers can or should do to influence the magnitude of these effects; they are a natural consequence of using material and other production inputs more efficiently. That said, *policy can influence the composition (and therefore the environmental footprint) of the rebound effect by ensuring that the full social costs of production and consumption are reflected in market prices.*

Notes

1 Consider the exemptions that large carbon emitting sectors – steel and agriculture for example – receive in some emissions trading schemes

2 This issue is aggravated in certain sectors – apparel and clothing for example – by fast moving consumer trends. Research undertaken in the United Kingdom indicates that the average consumer spends GBP 1 700 on clothes annually, but that around 30% of the clothes that are already owned have not been used for one year (WRAP, 2017[125]).

References

OECD (2018), *Fisheries Support Estimate*, http://www.oecd.org/tad/fisheries/fse.htm (accessed on 17 September 2018). [4]

OECD (2018), *International Trade and the Transition to a More Resource Efficient and Circular Economy*, https://one.oecd.org/document/COM/TAD/ENV/JWPTE(2017)3/REV3/en/pdf (accessed on 17 September 2018). [7]

OECD (2017), *Economic Features of Chemical Leasing*, https://one.oecd.org/document/ENV/JM/MONO(2017)10/en/pdf (accessed on 13 September 2018). [1]

OECD (2017), *MAPPING SUPPORT FOR PRIMARY AND SECONDARY METAL PRODUCTION*, https://one.oecd.org/document/ENV/EPOC/WPRPW(2016)2/FINAL/en/pdf (accessed on 13 September 2018). [3]

OECD (2016), *OECD'S PRODUCER SUPPORT ESTIMATE AND RELATED INDICATORS OF AGRICULTURAL SUPPORT Concepts, Calculations, Interpretation and Use*, http://www.oecd.org/tad/agricultural-policies/full%20text.pdf (accessed on 17 September 2018). [5]

OECD (2015), *OECD Companion to the Inventory of Support Measures for Fossil Fuels 2015*, OECD Publishing, Paris, http://dx.doi.org/10.1787/9789264239616-en. [2]

Wijkman, A., K. Skånberg and M. Berglund (2016), "The Circular Economy and Benefits for Society Jobs and Climate Clear Winners in an Economy Based on Renewable Energy and Resource Efficiency", http://www.clubofrome.org/wp-content/uploads/2016/03/The-Circular-Economy-and-Benefits-for-Society.pdf (accessed on 23 April 2018). [6]

Annex A. Case examples

Circular supply models: furniture manufacturing at Nico Spacecraft (from National Zero Waste Council, 2015 ([11]))

Nico Spacecraft designs and builds furniture, cabinetry and interiors for the residential market. Drawing from their global experience, the owners seek their inspiration in quality, good design and environmental principles. Plywood is a primary building material, so they sought out a plywood product in harmony with their environmental ethic: Purebond® by Columbia Forest Products. Nico Spacecraft has found that the PureBond® plywood they now use in most of their projects satisfies their quality, design and environmental criteria. They also use reclaimed materials where they can. Through seeking out circular supplies for their small business, Nico Spacecraft has been able to successfully incorporate circular economy practices such as non-toxic materials, design for recycling and durability into their products.

Nico Spacecraft's circular economy commitments are demonstrated in these other wood reuse efforts:

Urban sourcing of local trees: Every few years the company comes across an opportunity to salvage trees. If the species is right, they load, mill, stack and dry it. For example, a heritage white Oak tree had to be taken down for safety reasons. The wood was used for furniture and millwork for clients.

Recycled wood: Nino Spacecraft uses recycled wood for about 20% of its projects, sourced from professional salvage companies or directly from client homes. For example, first growth fir from old buildings such as a warehouse, school, shipyard and saw mill has been used to make furniture. In one unique case outdated heirloom furniture made of wood now on the endangered species list was taken apart, milled and re-glued into a contemporary look. In another case, clients were about to discard all their first growth Douglas Fir door frames. Nicospacecraft salvaged and stored them for the right project to come along.

Closed loop: with the exception of plastic packaging and five to six gallons a year of lacquer thinner which are returned to local recycling facilities, the company has a closed loop production process. The company reuses as much of the plastic packaging as it can in its own processes.

Circular supply models: Cradle-to-Cradle® at Tarkett

Tarkett is a leading manufacturer floor covering solutions operating globally around the world. Desso, a Tarkett brand for carpet tiles, provides high-quality carpets for commercial and domestic use, supplying inter alia the commercial, hospitality, maritime, and airline sector.

In 2008, prior to the acquisition by Tarkett, Desso launched a corporate strategy based on circularity principles which led to a Cradle-to-Cradle® gold level certification in 2015. In order to obtain a Cradle-to-Cradle® certification, the use of circular supplies is only the first step. Beyond material health and material reutilisation, there are also high standards with regards to renewable energy and carbon management, as well as, water stewardship and social fairness.

Desso is currently about to close its value chain completely. Milestones on this journey were its recyclable carpet tile backing called EcoBase™, its ReStart® collection program of old carpets, its Refinity® process , a recycling process which separates the yarn and other fibres from the backing, currently being re-built to process the post-consumer materials more efficiently. Desso is using recycled yarn known as ECONYL® as an input material for new carpets. Desso Cradle to Cradle Gold certified EcoBase™ backing is fully recyclable in Desso own production facility. The figure below depicts an illustration of Desso's technical cycle.

Figure A.1. The Desso technical cycle

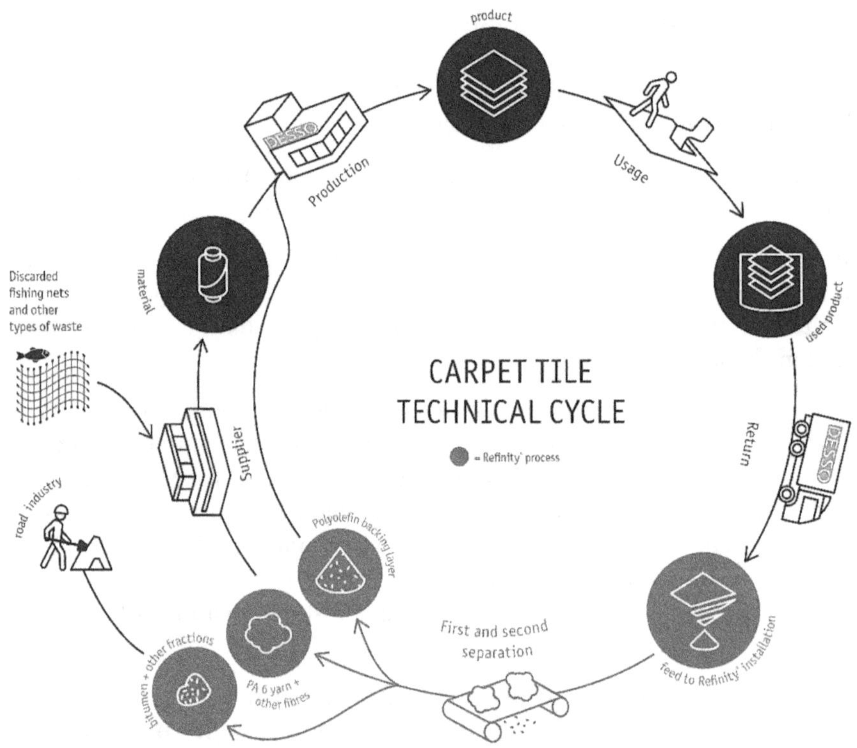

Source: EPEA (2017[2]), *EPEA – the Cradle of Cradle to Cradle*, https://bit.ly/2xk60LD

Resource recovery models: Industrial Symbiosis in Denmark

The Kalundborg Symbiosis industrial park is located 100km west from the Danish capital Copenhagen. It is perhaps one of the best-known examples for successfully putting the industrial symbiosis concept into practice. As a complete closed-loop industrial ecosystem it enables firms to directly sell materials, water, and energy to each other. This does not only reduce waste and pollution, it also saves money and generates additional income for the participating firms. See also the figure below for an illustration of the Kalundborg Symbiosis site.

Figure A.2. The Kalundborg Symbiosis Industrial Park

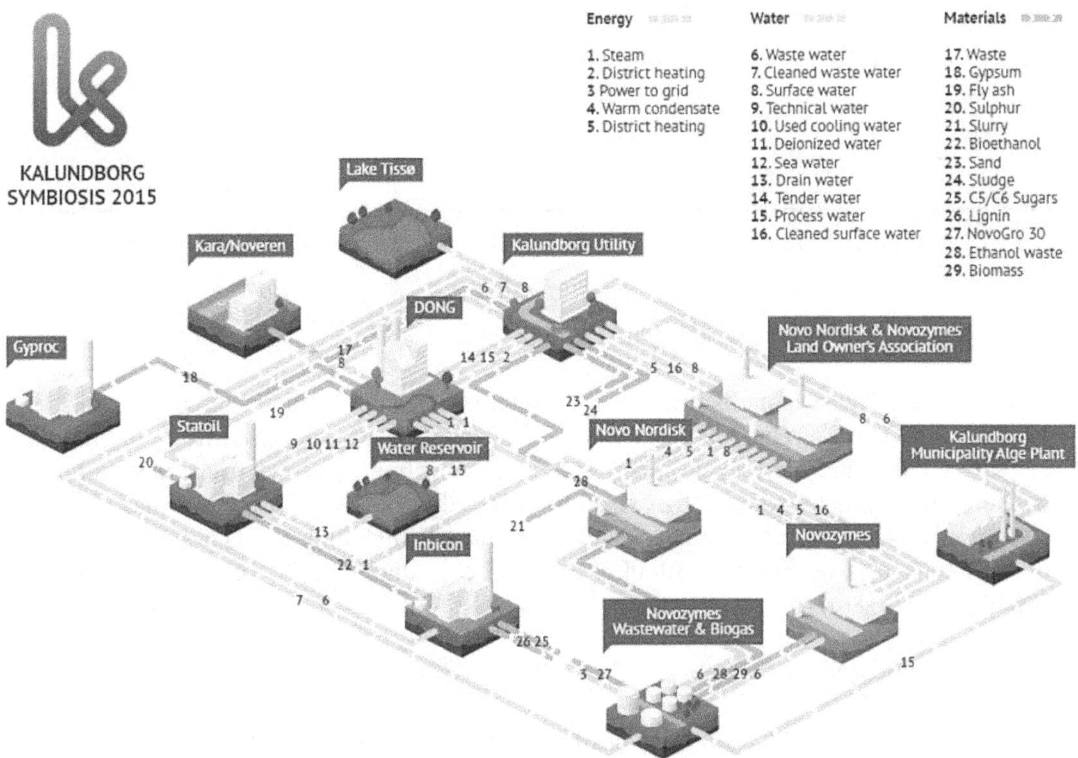

Source: Kalundborg Symbiosis (2018[3]), *Kalundborg Symbiosis Industrial Park,* https://bit.ly/2wCqsJI

The eco-industrial park's dense web of pipelines and symbiotic relationships between firms of different industries has gradually developed over time. The earliest cooperation between the municipality of Kalundborg and Statoil's (former Esso) in 1961 marked the starting point for this large-scale industrial experiment. The current park still features the local municipality together with eight other companies. Among them are the world's biggest insulin producer (Novo Nordisk), the world's biggest enzyme producer (Novozymes), the largest water treatment plant in Northern Europe (Kalundborg Forsyning), and the world's first bio-ethanol demonstration facility (Dong Energy).

In terms of the environmental benefits, Kalundborg Symbiosis manages to achieve significant resource savings for its participating entities. The table below lists a number of key resources and emission that can be avoided each year, such as water, biomass, and air pollutants.

Table A.1. Annual environmental benefits of Kalundborg Symbiosis Industrial Park

Resource / emission flow	Annual savings
Ground water	2.9 million m³
Surface water	1 million m³
Liquid sulphur	20 000 tonnes
Biomass	319 000 m³
Biomass (yeast slurry)	42 500 tonnes
CO2 emissions	64 460 tonnes
SO2 emissions	53 tonnes
Nox emissions	89 tonnes
Waste water	200 000 m³
Gypsum	170 000 tonnes

Source: Domenech and Davies (2011[4]), *Structure and morphology of industrial symbiosis networks: The case of Kalundborg,* https://bit.ly/2QIHgVx

Resource recovery models: upcycling at FREITAG

FREITAG is a Swiss manufacturer of bags, accessories, and clothing founded in 1993 by Markus and Daniel Freitag. The company produces its bags from used truck tarpaulins, car safety belts, and old bicycle inner tubes. By upcycling these materials, new value is created from what would otherwise be discarded waste. FREITAG has gained considerable scale in recent decades, each year around 400 000 products are produced out of 460 tons of truck tarps, 130 000 car seatbelts, and 12 000 bicycle inner tubes (FREITAG, 2018[5]).

Product life extension models: remanufacturing at Caterpillar

Caterpillar is the world industry leader of construction and mining equipment, diesel and natural gas engines, industrial gas turbines and diesel electric locomotives. Its brand "Cat® Reman" sells exclusively remanufactured products and is currently employing around 4 000 people in 17 locations worldwide (Lacy and Rutqvist, 2015[6]). In 2014, Caterpillar remanufactured more 2 million components with associated material savings of 75 400 tons (Waste Management World, 2016[7]).

As a manufacturer of capital intensive machinery, remanufacturing makes sense from a business perspective: Around 65% of its operating expenses are already material-related (Ellen Macarthur Foundation, 2016[8]). Caterpillar then sells its remanufactured products at a discount compared to new ones, but with an identical warranty. Still, it is more profitable to sell a remanufactured product than a brand new one, in particular when it is leased out. Then gross profits can be up to 2.75 times higher than selling original equipment (Lacy and Rutqvist, 2015[6]).

Remanufacturing at Caterpillar is also desirable from an environmental perspective. Around 86% less energy is consumed during remanufacturing compared to producing a new product from virgin material. Remanufacturing a cylinder head, for example, uses 86% less energy, 93% less water, and emits 61% less GHGs (Snodgress, 2012[9]).

Sharing models: sharing at the Toronto Tool Library (from the National Zero Waste Council (2015[1]))

Toronto Tool Library is a non-profit social enterprise that lends specialized tools to community members. The Tool Library's members borrow tools in the same way they would borrow a library book. The Tool Library has over 3 000 tools available for loan including home repair, construction and renovation, gardening and landscaping, and bicycle repair tools. The tools range from simple screw drivers and drills, to table saws, welding equipment, power generators. Four 3-D printers and a laser cutter are available for use onsite. The library is a money- and space-saving alternative to ownership. Tool sharing reduces consumption and waste. The philosophy of the library – and what sets it apart as a social enterprise – is that it is not trying to maximize profit but trying to maximize membership and access.

In early 2013, Toronto Tool Library posted a call for tool and financial donations on the internet and through the local media. The request went viral and the Library received over 1 000 tools. Subsequently, the library was able to build its inventory primarily through donations. The donated tools not only created a community asset, but put unused goods back in circulation and kept them out of the landfill. The Tool Library secured space for their first location in the basement of a recreation centre. About 100 volunteers participated in the initial renovations to convert a basement storage space into a community hub for sharing tools. The Tool Library also received USD 8 000 in donations to cover renovation costs. For inventory and membership management they used MyTurn's tool lending library software which was available for free. The business community also provided start-up support. For example, Canadian Tire and The Mibro Group donated tools and the local Salvation Army offered $5 thrift store discounts to tool donors.

The Tool Library has incubated other circular economy sharing services, from a kitchen library to a repair café and swapping. These help foster public acceptance of the sharing concept.

The Kitchen Library lends expensive and rarely used kitchen appliances to its members, and offers cooking and baking workshops. It operated out of the Tool Library's premises in its first year before relocating to space closer to high-density living, a move expected to enhance its viability.

The Repair Café is a monthly event held in partnership with several community groups such as the Toronto Public Library in which people bring and repair their broken appliances. By repairing rather than discarding broken appliances, participants extend the life of their goods, reduce further consumption and landfill waste and save money.

To further reduce consumption and waste, and promote its sharing philosophy, the Tool Library runs swapping events, such as an Alternative Christmas gift fair in which people bring and swap lightly used or new items considered giftable. Similar events are held for other high consumption holidays such as Halloween and Valentines – shifting the public norm from buying to swapping.

Sharing models: sharing at Peerby

Sharing models have become increasingly popular in recent years. One major catalyst for this development was the last financial and economic crisis starting in 2007 which led to higher unemployment rates and less purchasing power, especially among young people. In this changed context, it became more attractive to share existing goods rather than buying brand new ones. Other factors that have contributed to the rise of peer-to-peer renting communities are lower entry barriers for creating and hosting online platforms, as well as a cultural shift in consumer mentality towards more sustainability (EPRS, 2016[10]).

Durable household goods are underutilised assets that can be shared relatively easy. The Dutch platform Peerby started in 2012, specializing in these kinds of transactions between peers. Since then they have expended from their home market in the Netherlands to Belgium, France, Germany, and the US. More than 15 000 members are participating in the network either via the desktop version on their computer or via the mobile app (TechCrunch, 2013[11]). An advantage compared to similar platforms of this kind is that borrowers do not have to actively search for someone in the network who owns that item. Instead a borrowing request will be pushed to 100 people in close proximity. This way, 80% of all requests are apparently fulfilled within 30 minutes of their posting. Peer-review and rating systems ensure that the community remains highly quality and responsive.

Peerby is completely free for its members, while receiving funding support from the DOEN Foundation, Clinton Foundation, and Sanoma Media (Lacy and Rutqvist, 2015[6]). At the same time, the platform is testing several premium options for members, such as subscription plans for high-value item and opt-in insurances.

Product Service System models: light as a service at Philips

Philips started to experiment with the ESCO business model after being approached by one of its clients, the German architect Thomas Rau. Both sides agreed on a specific outcome: an exact level of brightness for Mr Rau's architect's office in Amsterdam. It was left to Philips how to achieve this goal with the most cost-effective solution. Philips would also retain ownership of its lighting equipment, being in charge of the installation, maintenance, upgrades, and end-of-life recovery. By applying the newest lighting technology – light-emitting diode (LED) lights – Philips was able to cut the energy costs of the architect's office by 35%.

After this successful project, Philips then reached out to public clients and approached the city of Washington, DC. The company offered to replace over 13 000 light fixtures in the city's parking garage with LED lights at no cost to the city. Only afterwards, Philips would earn money as a portion of the projected energy savings. The replacement was forecasted to reduce the energy usage by 68% or 15 million kWatt hours per year, resulting in $2 million in annual savings. It was estimated that these savings will remove over 11 000 metric tons of CO2 from the environment which is equivalent to removing over 2 300 cars from the road (Lacy and Rutqvist, 2015[6]; Philips, 2013[12])

The case of Philips shows that there are large environmental and economic benefits from upgrading existing lighting infrastructures. The global potential of this practice can be further illustrated by referring to the *Enlighten Initiative* which is a public/private partnership between the United Nations Environment Program, OSRAM, and Philips

Lighting, with the support of the Global Environment Facility. The website states that the share of electricity used for lighting accounts for around 15% of global energy consumption and for 5% of global greenhouse gas emissions. By switching to efficient on-grid and off-grid solutions, more than $140 billion could be saved every year, reducing CO2 emissions by 580 million tons annually (U4E, 2018[13]).

Product Service System models: access to rather than ownership of garments at Rent Frock Repeat (from the National Zero Waste Council (2015[1]))

Rent frock repeat is a Toronto-based online dress rental service that ships across Canada via Canada Post. The company offers members designer dress rentals through its e-commerce site as an alternative to purchasing expensive dresses that are rarely used. The company shops for the best designer dresses from around the world, visiting top fashion shows and showrooms, and then makes the dresses available for a fraction of the retail price. Customers save time, money and space and look fabulous at their events.

Technology makes the business possible and attention to their customers' needs make it popular. Over 57 000 on-line users browse the company's website for the perfect dress for their big night out. To help customers find the perfect dress on-line the company includes styling tips for a variety of occasions and body types. They have all sizes from 0-24 and customers can rent a second size for only $10 to ensure fit. Members also have access to private fitting appointments in the Toronto and Ottawa areas, private parties and phone or Skype consultations.

The business model has really struck a chord with customers and investors. Rent frock Repeat raised $1.15 million from two Ottawa-based angel investors in November 2014. A wise investment when you consider that it is estimated that 40% of Canadians are sharers and predict that the Sharing Economy is expected to double in the next year; Companies that embrace sharing will win loyal customer and increase market share. The angel investor funding allows Rent Frock Repeat to respond the growing popularity of dress rentals in Canada by opening up new storefronts. RfR is scheduled to open its Ottawa store in summer 2015 and plans to open a store in Calgary as well.

References

Domenech, T. and M. Davies (2011), "Structure and morphology of industrial symbiosis networks: The case of Kalundborg", *Procedia - Social and Behavioral Sciences*, Vol. 10, pp. 79-89, http://dx.doi.org/10.1016/J.SBSPRO.2011.01.011. [4]

Ellen Macarthur Foundation (2016), *Design and business model considerations for heavy machinery remanufacturing*, https://www.ellenmacarthurfoundation.org/case-studies/design-and-business-model-considerations-for-heavy-machinery-remanufacturing (accessed on 18 September 2018). [8]

EPEA (2017), *EPEA - the cradle of cradle to cradle*, https://www.epea.com/references/tarkett/ (accessed on 18 September 2018). [2]

EPRS (2016), "The Cost of Non-Europe in the Sharing Economy", http://dx.doi.org/10.2861/26238. [10]

FREITAG (2018), *Facts & Figures*, https://www.freitag.ch/en/support/factsandfigures (accessed on 18 September 2018). [5]

Kalundbord Symbiosis (2018), *Kalundborg Symbiosis Industrial Park*, http://www.symbiosis.dk/en/ (accessed on 18 September 2018). [3]

Lacy, P. and J. Rutqvist (2015), *Waste to wealth : the circular economy advantage.* [6]

National Zero Waste Council (2015), *CIRCULAR ECONOMY CASE STUDIES AND SNAPSHOTS 2*, http://www.nzwc.ca (accessed on 18 September 2018). [1]

Philips (2013), *Washington Metro Goes Green & Saves Green with Philips Performance Lighting Contract, Delivering on Sustainability Goals with 15 Million kWh Saved Annually*, https://www.usa.philips.com/a-w/about/news/archive/standard/news/press/2013/20131112-Philips-WMATA.html (accessed on 18 September 2018). [12]

Snodgress, D. (2012), *Remanufacturing - sustainability for the 21st Century*, https://www.wto.org/english/forums_e/public_forum12_e/session40snodgress_e.pdf (accessed on 18 September 2018). [9]

TechCrunch (2013), *Peerby's Local Lending App Is Ready To Help Neighbours Participate In The Sharing Economy*, https://techcrunch.com/2013/09/29/peerbys-local-lending-app-is-ready-to-help-neighbours-participate-in-the-sharing-economy/ (accessed on 18 September 2018). [11]

U4E (2018), *Lighting - United for Efficiency*, https://united4efficiency.org/products/lighting/ (accessed on 18 September 2018). [13]

Waste Management World (2016), "Remanufacturing - The Cat With Nine Lives", https://waste-management-world.com/a/in-depth-remanufacturing-the-cat-with-nine-lives (accessed on 18 September 2018). [7]

ORGANISATION FOR ECONOMIC CO-OPERATION AND DEVELOPMENT

The OECD is a unique forum where governments work together to address the economic, social and environmental challenges of globalisation. The OECD is also at the forefront of efforts to understand and to help governments respond to new developments and concerns, such as corporate governance, the information economy and the challenges of an ageing population. The Organisation provides a setting where governments can compare policy experiences, seek answers to common problems, identify good practice and work to co-ordinate domestic and international policies.

The OECD member countries are: Australia, Austria, Belgium, Canada, Chile, the Czech Republic, Denmark, Estonia, Finland, France, Germany, Greece, Hungary, Iceland, Ireland, Israel, Italy, Japan, Korea, Latvia, Lithuania, Luxembourg, Mexico, the Netherlands, New Zealand, Norway, Poland, Portugal, the Slovak Republic, Slovenia, Spain, Sweden, Switzerland, Turkey, the United Kingdom and the United States. The European Union takes part in the work of the OECD.

OECD Publishing disseminates widely the results of the Organisation's statistics gathering and research on economic, social and environmental issues, as well as the conventions, guidelines and standards agreed by its members.

OECD PUBLISHING, 2, rue André-Pascal, 75775 PARIS CEDEX 16
(97 2019 03 1 P) ISBN 978-92-64-31141-1 – 2019

www.ingramcontent.com/pod-product-compliance
Lightning Source LLC
LaVergne TN
LVHW081411110826
845149LV00010B/1711